Key Themes in Policing

Series editors: **Megan O'Neill**, University of Dundee, **Marisa Silvestri**, University of Kent, and **Stephen Tong**, Kingston University

---

The Key Themes in Policing series is designed to fill a growing need for titles which reflect the importance of incorporating 'research informed policing' and engaging with evidence-based policing within Higher Education curricula.

Also available

Challenges in Mental Health and Policing
By **Ian Cummins**

Towards Ethical Policing
By **Dominic Wood**

Critical Perspectives on Police Leadership
By **Claire Davis** and **Marisa Silvestri**

Police Occupational Culture
By **Tom Cockroft**

Policing the Police
By **Michael Rowe**

Miscarriages of Justice
By **Sam Poyser, Angus Nurse,** and **Rebecca Milne**

Key Challenges in Criminal Investigation
By **Martin O'Neill**

Plural Policing
By **Colin Rogers**

Understanding Police Intelligence Work
By **Adrian James**

Find out more at

policy.bristoluniversitypress.co.uk/key-themes-in-policing

Coming soon

Investigating and Policing Rape
By **Emma Williams**

Find out more at
policy.bristoluniversitypress.co.uk/key-themes-in-policing

PRACTICAL PSYCHOLOGY FOR POLICING

Jason Roach

First published in Great Britain in 2023 by

Policy Press, an imprint of
Bristol University Press
University of Bristol
1–9 Old Park Hill
Bristol
BS2 8BB
UK
t: +44 (0)117 374 6645
e: bup-info@bristol.ac.uk

Details of international sales and distribution partners are available at
policy.bristoluniversitypress.co.uk

British Library Cataloguing in Publication Data
A catalogue record for this book is available from the British Library

ISBN 978-1-4473-2591-8 hardcover
ISBN 978-1-4473-2592-5 paperback
ISBN 978-1-4473-2594-9 ePub
ISBN 978-1-4473-2593-2 ePdf

Cover design: Andrew Corbett
Front cover image: Branko Devic/Alamy Stock Photo
Bristol University Press and Policy Press use environmentally responsible print partners.
Printed and bound in Great Britain by CMP, Poole

To Robin and Sarah Bryant

Contents

Series preface

Megan O'Neill, Marisa Silvestri and Stephen Tong

The *Key Themes in Policing Series* aims to provide relevant and useful books to support the growing number of policing modules on both undergraduate and postgraduate programmes. The series also aims to support all those interested in policing from criminology, law, and policing students and policing professionals to those who wish to join policing services. It seeks to respond to the call for research in relevant and under-researched areas in policing encouraged by organisations such as the College of Policing in England and Wales. By producing a range of high-quality, research-informed texts on important areas in policing, contributions to the series support and inform both professional and academic policing curriculums.

Representing the tenth publication in the series, *Practical Psychology for Policing* by Jason Roach considers how, in the increasingly complex environment of contemporary policing, knowledge of practical psychology is becoming ever more important in everyday policing encounters, situations, and contexts. This book suggests how new ways of applying psychological knowledge and research can be of benefit in a range of policing contexts, for example, beat patrols, preventing crime, and using the Self-Selection Policing approach to uncover serious criminality from less serious offences. Jason Roach suggests how psychological knowledge, research, and policing might evolve together, to meet the changing challenges faced by contemporary policing.

Jason Roach is Professor of Psychology and Policing, and Associate Director for the Applied Criminology Centre at the University of Huddersfield, where he conducts crime and policing related research and works with police on serious crime. He has also appeared in the media discussing crime and policing related issues, published more than 25 academic articles, and co-written three books.

List of figures, tables, and boxes

Figure

Tables

Boxes

Acknowledgements

In the acknowledgements section of his autobiography, the comedian Jack Dee states that he has nobody to acknowledge, as he did everything himself.

Much as I would love to say the same here, my claim would be incredibly false as there are a lot of people that I both want and need to thank that have helped me with this book (in one way or another). Too many indeed to list here, so I will only thank the superstars individually.

First, I must thank the series editors, Steve, Megan, and Marisa and along with Freya and Rebecca at Policy Press, for their continued patience with me. Steve, I'm guessing that you had to put your neck on the line for me, and I hope I have gone some way to repaying your faith (or stupidity depending on which way you look at it).

Second, I would like to thank my friend, hero, and collaborator, Professor Ken Pease, who acts as my 'ideas midwife', as he very kindly suggests which of my ideas are worthy of being born and which ones need to stay in my head. For years I have blamed Ken for our book manuscripts always being late to the publisher. Ken, considering that I wrote this one alone, publicly, I absolve you of any blame for our previous tardiness – it was all me.

Third, I would like to thank my colleagues at Huddersfield particularly; Ash, Mel, Liam, and Rachel, and a special mention for Alan who has accompanied me on numerous 'field trips' and helped with the referencing for this book. Thank you all.

Fourth, I would like to thank my family for generally putting up with me. Perhaps now the other parents in the school playground will see that I do actually have a job, even though I often appear to be at my kids' school almost much as the teachers.

Fifth, I would like to thank Al Murray, Lauren Poultney, and Andy Hill for their comments on previous drafts. Your comments were invaluable, especially in my attempts to reach out to police and police staff.

Last, I would like to thank all the police officers and staff who I have worked with over the last 20 years, without whose kindness and patience I would not have had any material to write with. I have come to view policing to be one of the hardest jobs in the world. I hope this is not made even harder by constant interruptions by that bloke from Huddersfield University and his peculiar ideas and bizarre requests for help.

I thank you all. Much love.

Jason

1

Introduction (or unleashing the kraken)

Let us be clear from the start. I am not, nor ever have been, a police officer or indeed even been directly employed by any police service. This book therefore neither comprises a collection of war stories from experiences on the front line, nor provides a prescriptive list of how officers should behave in certain situations. It does, however, bring applied research which I (and colleagues) have conducted in crime and policing over the past two decades, into one convenient book.

I hope that this book will not be perceived as having been written by a patronising academic, as that really was not my intention. In fact, any egg-sucking caused (to grannies or anyone else) by reading this book, was completely unintended and please accept my sincere apologies if it comes across so.

If the often trotted-out opinion that it takes five years for a police officer to acquire the knowledge and experience needed to be a police officer (provenance unknown) rings true in any way, this book will hopefully make a contribution to the expediting of both, by presenting practical examples of how a little psychological knowledge and research can be applied in policing.

Although this book was principally written with those new to policing in mind, both newly 'sworn' 'front-line' police officers and police staff (such as those working in prevention or supporting criminal investigations), more 'experienced' readers or those familiar with academic research in this area will hopefully also take some learning or ideas from it.

This book represents my take on how an introduction to how some psychological research and theory can be used to inform various policing tasks (and vice-versa). The first aim is to demonstrate how a little knowledge of psychology can be used in the understanding and practice of policing; namely, its application for the policing tasks of *crime prevention*, *street patrols*, and *criminal investigation*. Although the psychological research drawn on here and applied to such policing tasks is arguably limited, one hopes that this book in some way will act as a catalyst for the production of further books focusing on how psychology can be used in other aspects of policing, such as cybercrime and counter-terrorism policing.

A second aim for this book is to show how policing and academic research can become 'welcome bedfellows' sharing ideas and evidence via a two-way exchange to enhance policing practice and knowledge. Indeed, I have taken so long in getting around to starting this book that the UK Society for Evidence-Based Policing (SEBP), which is at the forefront of exactly this in the UK, has rather stolen what little thunder I might have mustered up. My self-rationalisation, however, is not to regret another career-defining opportunity missed, but to point out that this book focuses on practical psychology for policing and not evidence-based methods per se, although evidence-based examples are presented whenever and wherever possible.

I know that I have rather a lot of different types of hope for this book, but another one is that by reading it psychology, criminology, and police studies students will realise that complex experimentation and difficult-to-understand theory is not always the best way in which to assist those engaged with the infinitely difficult task of policing. For me, the popular misperception that the role of academics is to make that which is easily understood, so complicated so that it ceases to be so, does not ring true. Occam's Razor states that the simplest is often the most effective explanation, mainly because it is easier to understand and so remember. Simple for me wins the prize every time.

At the risk of serving up what might be misconstrued a platitude (which it genuinely is not meant to be), my mantra has always been that research is something done with, and not to, those in policing. To this end, I have tried to write this book in the most welcoming and engaging way possible, which, with the occasional drift into anecdotes of my own based on my experience of 20 years of research in crime and policing, arguably separates it from the usual style and format adopted by most textbooks.

We begin with what might first appear to be a self-indulgent and nostalgic story, but please bear with it as its relevance to the aims and objectives of this book will hopefully become apparent.

Psychology, tacit knowledge, and how to control the classroom mob

Looking back, one of the early positive influencers (in the non-social media sense of the word as it was the 1980s) of my adolescence was my English literature teacher, Mr Graham Davies, or Mr D as we affectionately called him (although not to his face). This teacher extraordinaire was not only dead trendy, into cool music, and popular with female members of staff (three things all teenage lads aspire to be), but he also possessed a seemingly magical talent for noticing which child(ren) in his class was talking or messing about, before they had actually begun to do so – a kind of Tom Cruise in 'Minority Report'[1] type character, ready to arrest us before we'd even committed the crime. His most famous pre-emptive strike (or pre-cog, in 'Minority Report' speak) was when he told a boy off for messing about, while actually having his back to the class because he was writing on the blackboard. I thought this was brilliant and how he was able to do this perplexed me for some weeks, until it finally dawned on me – he always noticed who was just about to talk or was most likely to mess about (there was a shortlist of repeat offenders) just before he turned his back, but kept quiet until *we* thought he could not see us. I could not keep my new hypothesis to myself and had to ask Mr D whether my observation was correct or whether he truly was some kind of magician or psychic? He said that he would only tell me the answer to my question if I promised not to tell my classmates. I agreed to his terms. I was right. He said that when he was doing his teacher training, he had observed a teacher using the exact same tactic and had been equally mystified. He went on to say that after the lesson the said teacher told him how he had done it (just as he had with me) and that it would become one of the most valuable classroom tactics he would ever use in his future teaching career. He said that, unfortunately, I probably wouldn't need it in any career that I might have, which I took at the time to be a compliment – that he thought that I was destined for bigger and better things than simply teaching English. On reflection, I might have got the exact reverse meaning of what he meant and, looking at what I call my career, he may well have been right!

Undoubtedly a brilliant classroom tactic, but what relevance does it have for improving police and policing performance on the streets of Britain? To be clear, I am not advocating that police officers should turn their backs on criminals in a similar way as that would be at best ridiculous and at worst dangerous. This story is simply a metaphor for the purpose of this book. Decades ago, and without even knowing it, Mr Davies had identified two important themes for this book; *tacit knowledge* (knowledge of how to do something gained from experience of doing it) and an ability to *predict likely behaviour from observable cues*. What this great teacher had done was pass on to me a valuable piece of 'tacit knowledge' – don't tell someone off until you turn your back to a class, and they will be less likely to chance misbehaving in future. Much of this book is about sharing the learning of how to do various aspects of policing, such as identifying active, serious criminals from the minor offences they commit (for example, Roach, 2007).

In his book *The Tacit Dimension*, Michael Polyanyi (1966) suggests that 'we *can know more than we can tell*' (1966, p 4, emphasis added), with tacit knowledge being 'Knowledge that is informally acquired rather than explicitly taught and allows a person to succeed in certain environments and pursuits. It is stored without awareness and therefore is not easily articulated' (*American Association of Psychology Dictionary*).[2] In Mr D's case, how to make a class think that you have eyes in the back of his head.

What remains a constant source of frustration for me is that although knowledge of standard police procedures and criminal law are passed on to police officers in the form of textbooks and guidance notes (and quite rightly so), how to 'actually do something' is often left to chance that it will be passed on from one officer to another; however, sadly it is often not, and disappears forever into the annals of a career passed by, with a retiring police officer. As previously suggested, by definition, as such acquired knowledge by experience is often difficult to articulate, there is currently no means by which to effectively capture it, preserve it, store it, collate it, and make it freely available to all those in policing. In this sense, no 'corporate memory' of how to do policing exists in the UK (and I doubt anywhere else in the world). At best its transition from one cop to the next will be piecemeal and inconsistent, while at worst it will be non-existent or simply 'lost'. When and where the experience of actually doing something (that is, 'tacit knowledge') is passed onto the less experienced by the greater experienced, it is exponentially helpful; for example, how to spot someone acting suspiciously (a topic of focus in Chapter 6). 'Tragic' does not begin to describe the waste that occurs when it is not.

Alas, at the present time, no machinery currently exists by which retiring officers can upload their experience and knowledge to a massive 'corporate database'. Surely the passing on of policing knowledge (tacit and otherwise) should help expedite the 'experience' and 'knowledge' process, potentially helping save officer lives. This was a primary motivation for me to write this book.

This book in no way claims to be a panacea for all ills, it simply represents a modest attempt to provide those in policing (and those interested in it) with some 'how to knowledge-based tactics', supplied with a degree of theoretical and empirically tested support, for consideration in routine police duties and activities. I will refer to this as 'bottom-up' knowledge and learning.

The opposite to a 'bottom-up' approach of course is a 'top-down' one, and this book will also include the latter to compliment the former. Put simply, what I am referring to here is that knowledge that academic research has tested and provided evidence of efficacy which, if known about by more of those in policing, can help to make carrying out many routine tasks a little easier. For example, without doubt, one of the biggest practical contributions that psychological research has made to policing has been in the advancement of suspect interview techniques, with an abundance of literature on how best to conduct suspect interviews, much of which is discussed in Chapter 2. Interestingly, how best to interview witnesses and victims is still lagging behind by comparison, at least in terms of attention paid by academic researchers.

Although this book will primarily endeavour to suggest how psychological research can be used to help those charged with carrying out common, routine policing tasks, such as street patrols and dealing with the public, focus is also placed on practical psychology for criminal investigations.

About this book

For some unfathomable reason there are still not many books specifically about psychology and policing. Although now more than two decades' old, in my opinion Peter Ainsworth's *Psychology and Policing* (2002) remains the best. The present book is different to others in that it focuses on a number of different ways of integrating psychological research and knowledge into policing, and not on specific roles which psychologists play in policing, such as occupational psychologists or in the recruitment of officers and staff. This is not to 'dumb down' the significance of the contribution that psychology and psychologists have made to other areas of policing, but simply to re-iterate that this book's point of departure is by focusing instead on how psychology can help those involved with practical aspects of operational policing. Where other important areas of intersection between psychology and policing are omitted from this book, such as recruitment of police officers and organisational psychological aspects of policing organisations, are worthy of coverage elsewhere, they do not fit with the purpose of this book, and so are not.

At a risk of repeating myself, the point of departure for this book is that it focuses on the interaction of psychology and policing in different areas of policing and from different perspectives; namely, how the application of some basic psychology might help police think about, make decisions, and deal with different crime and policing problems, while at the same time helping to explain why it is that police as decision-makers think, act, and behave as they do. For example, how police might better identify those members of the public that give them a false address, when they are on patrol (Chapter 5).

This book begins by introducing the reader to how, and in different ways historically, that psychological research and policing have 'interacted', such as with the interviewing of suspects, or in crime prevention. It also suggests how policing would further benefit further from a wider application of psychological knowledge and research perhaps to less obvious, less focused on practical task-based areas of policing, such as identifying those giving false personal details, or how to spot and minimise cognitive bias in criminal investigations. Much of the research presented here has been carried out over the past decade by myself and colleagues, and to some extent represents a pooling of ideas and research on the topic in the one place. I did not start out with the intention of writing a 'semi-autobiography' and if indeed this has what it has become then I apologise, but I like to think that I am not done yet!

Within regard to how this book is structured, as stated the early focus of the book will be on some of the obvious ways in which psychology (that is, psychological research and knowledge) and policing have connected and evolved together, and the kind of relationship they have had, before moving swiftly on to chapters designed to highlight how psychological research can be employed in different aspects of contemporary policing.

Later chapters show how current psychological research can be applied practically in policing functions, such as criminal investigation and identifying active serious offenders from more minor infractions of the law, as well as more general issues such as how police decision-making can be improved by identifying and minimising the influence of common cognitive bias. Other chapters focus on aspects of policing, such as: developing police psychology for the street, interviewing witnesses and suspects, and employing psychological thinking and research to reduce and prevent crime.

As stated at the beginning of this Introduction, it was written deliberately in an as approachable way as I dare, so (hopefully) it is equally appropriate for academic as non-academic consumption (for example, police officers, police community support officers, other police staff, and those working in the offices of Police and Crime Commissioners). This is deliberately so for two reasons: first, often the best ideas are clear and simple and that way they stand more chance of being remembered and passed on; and, second, because it has a practical rather than academic purpose (that is, it is for those engaged in and interested in policing to use). Although the risk of falling off increases when you try to ride two horses at once, the structure of the chapters is such that the academic and practical sections, although fitting together, are easily distinguishable for the time-pressed police reader or student. That said, I do hope that, when convenient, readers will return to the parts they have neglected as soon as they have time. Each chapter also provides a space designed to encourage readers to critically reflect on the technique, approach, and evidence presented, with suggested reading provided at the end for the particularly 'eager beavers'.

Although this book focuses primarily on UK policing and police issues, various non-UK comparative examples will be provided where appropriate and the international reader is encouraged to draw similarities and comparisons where possible, and to use some of the knowledge acquired for practical crime and policing projects.[3]

Book structure

This book is divided into eight self-contained yet complimentary chapters, which do not necessarily have to be read in the order in which they are presented. Although ideally this book should be read in one sitting, when pragmatism and reality are taken into consideration, then this book is structured in such a way that students and policing practitioners can dip in and out, if and when time allows, or when specific crime and policing challenges necessitate.

Chapter 2 – Psychology and policing: welcome bedfellows?

This chapter briefly charts the history of the relationship between the discipline of psychology and the role and the function of policing in England and Wales. Rather like service station points on a motorway, specific areas in which where psychology has influenced and impacted on policing and how, will be explored including the police interviewing of suspects and witnesses, detecting lies and deception, offender profiling, and crime prevention. The chapter will hopefully provide an appropriate psychology and policing context for the remainder of the book, especially for those more unfamiliar with psychological theory and research.

Chapter 3 – Human and police decision-making

This chapter looks at how those involved with policing make decisions. The psychology of decision-making will be explored in a range of different contexts, including criminal investigation. The substantial research on cognitive bias, which can often serve to hinder rather than enhance human decision-making, is explored, and some suggestions are made for how its potentially catastrophic effect on police decision-making can be identified and minimised. Put simply, how we can help investigators avoid common biases because of 'being human'.

Chapter 4 – Challenging common police perceptions of career criminals and serious offenders

This deliberately short chapter provides the evidence base for police to view serious offenders as being *offence versatile* as opposed to *offence homogenous* (specialised) and why this is an important switch for those working in policing. This chapter challenges the current police perceptions of the offending patterns of serious criminals as offence homogenous or specialists, and provides evidence that they are instead offence *heterogenous*, being versatile and varied in the crimes that they commit. Evidence from contemporary research on criminal careers and criminal psychology is presented to establish the offence versatility of serious offenders, paving the way for more offender versatile-based approaches, such as *Self-Selection Policing* introduced in Chapter 5.

Chapter 5 – Self-Selection Policing

In this chapter the 'Self-Selection Policing' (for example, Roach, 2007a; Roach 2007b; Roach and Pease, 2016) approach is introduced whereby active, serious offenders can be detected by the small crimes they commit, such as parking illegally in accessible (disabled) parking bays, and driving while disqualified. Although still an emergent additional approach for identifying active, serious criminals by specific minor 'trigger' offences they commit, its adaption by police continues to grow but several important hurdles to its wider application are highlighted, with future research areas also suggested.

Chapter 6 – Psychology, expertise, and improving police officer street-craft

This chapter begins with a brief synopsis of the psychological literature relating to lies and deception, before moving to suggestions for how it can be used practically by police in everyday situations, such as how to spot liars in police–public street interactions. Research is presented which demonstrates how such knowledge can be applied practically, to better inform police how to detect those giving false addresses and dates of birth to them in face-to-face encounters. This chapter comprises both psychological knowledge and some excellent examples of tacit knowledge provided by serving and former police officers.

Chapter 7 – Psychology and crime prevention

This chapter will begin by charting how psychology has been used to help prevent and reduce crime since the early 1980s, with the advent of Situational Crime Prevention (Clarke, 1980) and environmental criminology, both rooted firmly within behavioural psychology. The bulk of the chapter will be more contemporary, focusing on the 'nudge' approach (Thaler and Sunstein, 2008) whereby a range of options are presented in such a way that it shapes behaviour in a desired direction, while still maintaining freedom of choice. Environmental nudges being at the often more subtle and cheaper end of Situational Crime Prevention and designed with the aim of maximum return for minimum effort and cost. How 'nudging' can be utilised to reduce crime is currently being explored (by me and colleagues) with several police forces in England and Wales and will be presented here. That said, a call for a wider perspective on influencing thinking (for example, Rotter's Locus of Control, 1966) and behaviour is made in terms of thinking about and introducing measures and interventions to prevent crime.

Chapter 8 – Psychology and police wellbeing

This chapter presents the growing importance of psychological research in understanding the effects of 'doing the job', on police personnel wellbeing, and subsequently helping to develop and provide more effective and more bespoke police support and support services. The point is made that as 'policing' is not a homogenous occupation, then there will be many different potentially negative wellbeing effects on those doing different roles and jobs within policing, and as such a 'one size fits all' supportive approach is an impossibility. Current research into potentially different negative wellbeing effects on criminal investigators involved with different types of criminal investigation (including homicide, sexual offences, and crime scene analysis) is presented, alongside commonly used coping strategies (such as good support from colleagues) and useful support services.

Chapter 9 – Psychology and policing: taking stock and where do we go from here?

This short chapter begins with a very brief reflection on the book, before moving to consideration of how psychological research and knowledge might evolve and transform to meet the new challenges that are faced by contemporary policing, with, for example, emergent crime arenas, such as the World Wide Web and how it presents a different area for both new and old types of crime to be committed and in different ways. Suggestions for further areas in research need are provided, including how police and academic researchers might best work in collaboration, and how police might avoid accusations of 'victim blaming' when implementing crime prevention initiatives.

Chapter format

Each chapter contains 'boxes' which provide more information on a specific theme, theory, aspect of research, or simply invite the reader to 'think for a minute'. Their reading is not vital to understanding what is being presented, but it is hoped that the reader will use their content as a way of clarifying and consolidating their learning.

Each chapter ends with suggestions for additional reading and websites for those interested in learning more on each chapter topic. I make no apology for the apparent 'old age' of some of the books and articles, because I do not believe that the best research and theory is necessarily the most recent research and theory. So please do not be put off by references from the last century as I have deliberately gone back to 'the classics' where I have thought it appropriate to do so.

2

Psychology and policing: welcome bedfellows?

Introduction

The purpose of this chapter is twofold: first, to demonstrate how psychological research and knowledge have contributed to the practice of policing (and vice versa) over the past few decades, by highlighting several areas where famously the relationship between psychology and specific aspects of policing has been most noticeable, and second, to provide a little introductory psychology for those readers not au fait with some of the psychological research and knowledge which has been applied in policing. Please don't feel that you will be at disadvantage – you won't be!

As this book is not about teaching police officers about psychology per se, this chapter will only present that psychological research (deemed by me) to be most relevant to and in policing, with only enough necessary psychological knowledge provided to enable readers to grasp the ways in which it has influenced policing and to provide a broader context from which to understand the remainder of the book. That said, we start at the beginning with science and crime or *crime science.*

Science and crime (or crime science)

'Crime science is the application of scientific methods and knowledge from many disciplines to the development of practical and ethical ways to reduce crime and increase security' (Wortley, Sidebottom, Tilley, and Laycock, 2019, p 2).

To the uninformed, disinterested, or both, the definition of *crime science*, provided by several of its principal architects, may echo that given for '*criminology*', but for some of those in the know there are several albeit subtle, yet significant, differences. First, crime scientists claim that criminology is actually not about crime at all, as it has a much broader remit on why people commit crime, the characteristics of offenders, the structure of the society in which crimes are committed, the formation and administration of the law, the function of the criminal justice system, and so on, and not on crime itself (Wortley et al, 2019). One does not need to look far for evidence to support such a claim; take a look at the content of a criminology degree provided by any UK university, and you will see that much of the content is not really about crime, but about power, law-making, and how to best to deal with and reform those that transgress it. Trust me, although I do not consider myself to be a 'criminologist', I have taught various aspects criminology for over 15 years now and I have made this point consistently during course review and development meetings, with admittedly little influence on what aspects of 'traditional criminology' I feel that students need to know most. I am not alone. End of short rant.

The Oxford online dictionary defines 'science' as knowledge about the structure and behaviour of the natural and physical world, based on facts that you can prove, for example by experiments, new developments in science and technology, the advance of modern science, and the laws of science.'[1]

Crime scientists claim that not all criminology can be considered 'scientific' as so defined. For example (and they don't mince their words) they suggest that when examined, the operation of the criminal justice system involves 'a great deal of policy and practice that is based on popular sentiment, ideology, political expediency, intuition, moralistic assumptions, "good ideas" and "what we have always done" rather than good science' (Wortley et al, 2019, p 1).

Crime science, on the other hand, is an 'evidence-based, problem-solving approach which embraces empirical research' (Wortley et al, 2019, p 1). The key words here being 'evidence-based' and 'empirical research'.

Although advocated and practiced as an approach by some for decades, it was only given the collective noun of crime science in the late 1990s by television presenter and journalist, Nick Ross. Crime science is an example of the application of a scientific thinking and principles to reducing crime and improving the effectiveness of policing and security.

To be fair, a vast majority of those considered to be the main architects of crime science in the UK hale from psychology backgrounds; for example, the broadcaster, Nick Ross has a psychology degree, Professor Gloria Laycock has a degree and PhD in psychology, as does my friend and erstwhile collaborator Professor Ken Pease OBE. This is probably explained by the lack of criminology undergraduate degrees available at UK universities until the late 1980s, before which they remained few and far between, and certainly were sparse when I was deliberating which degree to study for in 1989.

One of the principal reasons that the crime science approach was created was because these three protagonists (and others) recognised that although psychology and criminology are arguably the most obvious disciplines within which to understand crime and criminality, they are not individually (or even together) sufficient to prevent and reduce crime significantly. Hence, incorporating and employing a much broader range of scientific disciplines, such as engineering and computer science, to solving crime problems, as crime science strongly advocates.

For a host of different examples of the application of different crime and policing problems, the reader is directed to the Jill Dando Institute for Security and Crime Science, at University College London[2] and to the Center for Problem-Orientated Policing, at Arizona State University.[3] The Crime Science and Problem-Orientated Policing approaches to crime and policing are only briefly explored here, as they are discussed more fully in Chapter 7.

So that is science and crime, but more specifically, what about science and policing? Are they, for example, compatible partners and welcome bedfellows, or are they in any way incompatible? Let's start where science and policing definitely meet – forensic science.

Science and policing

We begin our exploration of this question at the most obvious place where policing and science interact – the application of 'forensic science' in criminal investigations.

Forensic science

The invention and advancement of forensic science is arguably still the most common place where policing and science interact. Put simply, forensic science is an umbrella term used to represent a variety of different scientific disciplines (for example, anthropology, geology, and entomology) and their application in the service of the law (that is, criminal investigation and the compiling of criminal evidence). The bedrock of all forensic science rests on Locard's Exchange Principle (1934), 'every contact leaves a trace', whether that be the trace of a suspected offender retrieved form a crime scene, or the trace of a crime scene on suspected offender (see, for example, Horswell and Fowler, 2004).

One early example of the application of forensic science to policing (and still used) is fingerprinting, but others include analysis of textile fibres, soil, hair, foliage, footwear impressions (for example, forensic podiatry), and the less savoury aspects of human biology – bodily fluids (for example, blood, saliva, and semen) commonly used to identify (or confirm) a suspect's identity; for example, by analysing DNA extracted from a crime scene. A snapshot of the contribution of DNA science to police investigations is presented briefly in Box 2.1.

So, if policing incorporates forensic science, then does this make policing more 'scientific'? We shall briefly look at this question next.

Box 2.1: DNA evidence and criminal investigation

Deoxyribonucleic acid (DNA) is the molecule that contains the genetic code of all organisms. It is in virtually in every cell of every organism, and, put simply, it tells cells what proteins to make. Sir Alec Jeffreys pioneered the first method of DNA profiling in the mid-1980s, known as Restriction Fragment Length Polymorphism (RFLP) to examine the repetitive regions in the human genome thereby providing an ability to identify individual people (see, for example, Roach and Pease, 2006). For this to be possible, molecules of DNA must be first extracted from the human tissue such as blood, skin, semen, and saliva.

The implications in forensic context were not realised until its use in the identification and conviction of Colin Pitchfork in 1987 for the rape and murder of two 15- year-old girls in Leicestershire in 1983 and 1986. The drawback with the early DNA profiling technique was that its use with small or degraded samples was minimal; indeed, in a presentation I witnessed over a decade ago, Sir Alec stated that originally you would have needed a bucket of saliva to be able to extract a DNA profile with any great degree of certainty. Not many criminals at that time (or indeed this) have ever been so obliging!

Since its first involvement in the case convicting Colin Pitchfork 30 years ago, advances in technology (Low Copy Number – LCN) have enabled the DNA profiling process to become much faster and more sensitive leading to its use in millions of criminal investigations around the world.

Although, many consider DNA profiling to be the 'gold standard' of forensic science it is not infallible; for example, it is transportable, it is not date-stamped so if found at a crime scene the individual may have been there innocently days, weeks, or even years before, and it does not by itself prove guilt if found at a crime scene (for a fuller discussion, see McCartney, 2006).

I never fail to stress the important point to students that although DNA evidence (and other forms of forensic evidence) may often compliment the criminal investigation process, they *do not replace it or render it unnecessary*. To solely depend on the application of science for the detection and conviction of serious criminals would very be dangerous for the detection process and criminal justice system as a whole (Roach and Pease, 2006). That said, forensic science does represent the most obvious historical example of policing and science interacting.

Policing: craft, science, a bit of both, and who cares?

According to the Cambridge online dictionary (please notice that I'm being fair and using a range of different online dictionaries), the noun 'craft' is defined as being 'Skill and experience, especially in relation to making objects; a job or activity that needs skill and experience, or something produced using skill and experience'.[4]

Traditionally, policing has been considered by most to be a 'craft', with appropriate skills, knowledge, and experience necessary to 'do the job', acquired primarily through 'doing the job'. Peter Stelfox, in his 2008 book *Criminal Investigation*, refers to the traditional view of police as being 'omnicompetent'; that is, able to do everything and anything that policing entails simply by gaining policing experience and the mentorship of senior officers.

Mercifully, over the past few decades this traditional view has been replaced with the common perception of policing as comprising a multitude and variety of different roles, contexts, and situations, for which different knowledge and skill sets are necessary and not simply the 'Swiss army knife' approach of the versatile, 'omnicompetent cop'. Indeed, in many areas of the world of policing, great efforts have been made to move perceptions of what policing is and the practice of doing policing away from being 'craft-based' to more of a 'science', best illustrated perhaps by the 'Evidence-Based Policing' (Sherman, 1998, 2013) approach, highlighted in Box 2.2.

Box 2.2: Evidence-Based Policing

The Evidence-Based Policing approach is very much the brainchild of Professor Lawrence Sherman, originally stemming from his paper, 'Evidence-Based Policing', published in the *Ideas in American Policing Series* (1998).

Based very much on Sherman's original definition, the UK College of Policing describes Evidence-Based Policing (EBP) as follows:

> In an Evidence-Based Policing approach, police officers and staff create, review and use the best available evidence to inform and challenge policies, practices and decisions.
>
> As a way of working, it can be supported by collaboration with academics and other partners.
>
> The 'best available' evidence will use appropriate research methods and sources for the question being asked. Research should be carefully conducted,

peer reviewed, and transparent about its methods, limitations, and how its conclusions were reached. The theoretical basis and context of the research should also be made clear. Where there is little or no formal research, other evidence such as professional consensus and peer review, may be regarded as the 'best available', if gathered and documented in a careful and transparent way.

Research can be used to:

- develop a better understanding of an issue – by describing the nature, extent and possible causes of a problem or looking at how a change was implemented; or
- assess the effect of a policing intervention – by testing the impact of a new initiative in a specific context or exploring the possible consequences of a change in policing.[5]

Evidence-Based Policing does not provide definitive answers that officers and staff should apply uncritically. Officers and staff will reflect on their practice, consider how the 'best available' evidence applies to their day-to-day work, and learn from their successes and failures. The approach should mean officers and staff can ask questions, challenge accepted practices, and innovate in the public interest. As will be suggested in a later discussion of problem-solving approaches to crime and policing, such as SARA (Scanning Analysis Response and Assessment) presented in Chapter 7, EBP is perhaps best seen as informing the 'response' element.

Source: Reproduced from the UK College of Policing website, available at https://whatworks.college.police.uk/About/Pages/What-is-EBP.aspx (accessed 3 July 2021).

For a decent collection of EBP examples, the interested reader is directed to the UK College of Policing[6] and Cambridge Institute of Criminology websites.[7]

Having now briefly looked at how arguably more scientific approaches have been adopted and even become embedded in contemporary policing (particularly in the UK), we now move to a short exploration of some of the most obvious ways in which psychology and psychological research have informed policing in similar ways. We begin with what we mean by psychology before moving swiftly to a sub-discipline of psychology, arguably most likely to contribute to policing – *forensic psychology*.

Psychology and policing

Let us start with the basics. Psychology is often described, by psychologists at least, as a 'science' (for example, Gross, 1996). I am reminded of the first departmental meeting I attended some 15 years ago, at my current university. As I was new to the job, I hadn't yet learnt that such meetings should be avoided at all costs, and how that sending 'your apologies' as soon as you are invited to a meeting is usually the best form of action. I have been much quicker off the mark ever since this event. All seemed to be progressing in a rather expectedly mundane and unexciting fashion, when one colleague, a psychology lecturer, announced that she had applied for 'chartered scientist status'. Well, for a couple of my sociologist and criminologist colleagues, that appeared to be the most ridiculously funny thing that they had ever heard. One responded by saying, "Psychology a science? Well, I've heard it all now." Which on reflection, was quite rude. With the touchpaper now lit, a massive debate/row ensued about whether psychology is actually a science and as such whether psychologists are actually scientists, chartered or otherwise. I had learned at this point that not all discussions between so-called academics are actually neither academic or indeed even discussions at all.

As a fully paid-up and proud psychologist (and with a Master of Science in Psychology) I of course felt, and still feel, very strongly that psychology is a science and that I too was therefore a scientist. However, I really couldn't be bothered getting involved in this conversation or even picking a team, so I made my excuses and left to give a lecture on 'offender profiling'. To this day I have never applied for 'chartered scientist status' and I'm not sure whether this is best explained by the aforementioned 'psychology is/is not a science incident', or whether I really don't care that much either way.

You might be thinking, what is the point of telling this story? Simply, that it might not be universally accepted that psychology is a science, but most psychologists believe that it is. Gross, for example, defines psychology as 'the science of mind and behaviour' (1996). For now, at least, and for the purposes of this book, we will take it that it is. But why might this be important to policing? Academic researchers and scholars over the past few decades have increasingly made the case that policing needs to be 'more scientific' in its approach and application (for example, the development of EBP (Sherman, 1998) and that psychological knowledge and research being 'scientific' can help with this transition. It can be argued, therefore, that they should make welcome bedfellows. Unlike my sociologist and psychologist colleagues of yester year, I hear you say! One obvious overlap of psychology and policing being forensic psychology.

Forensic psychology, forensic psychologists, and the rest of us

Ask a member of the UK or US public how a forensic psychologist helps police, and the most likely responses will either be 'offender profiling' or 'cracking open serious criminals' in suspect interview scenarios (Roach and Selby-Fell, forthcoming). Interestingly, although the general remit of psychologists working in policing in the UK over the past decade has expanded way beyond offender profiling and interviewing suspects, paradoxically, the work done by those calling themselves 'forensic psychologists' has appeared to be too narrow, as it is a title mainly used by psychologists who work with/treat criminals, mostly of the incarcerated variety. The most likely explanation for this being that forensic psychology in the UK has become more 'clinically orientated' over the past few decades, indeed all UK forensic psychologists must be registered with the National Health Council. Tautologically, this move has probably been driven by what forensic psychologists are considered to do most – reforming or rehabilitating convicted criminals in prison and probation (parole) settings. Forensic psychologists in the UK are often those referred previously referred to as 'prison psychologists' (Roach and Selby-Fell, forthcoming), leaving those of us not doing this type of work with a need to perhaps find a new collective noun(s) to suitably explain what we are, such as criminologist, crime scientist, or behavioural scientist. Although, on second thoughts, I'm not really one for labels, so we will leave it there.

Surprisingly, for although what constitutes a forensic psychologist in the UK may have perhaps contracted, in terms of what 'forensic psychology' constitutes as a discipline (for example, from looking at the content and syllabus of many UK Master's degree courses) does not appear to have followed suit. The British Psychological Society (BPS), the representative body for professional psychologists of all flavours and persuasions in the UK, for example, still describes forensic psychology in much broader terms than the application of psychology to reform and rehabilitate convicted criminals: 'Forensic psychology is the application of psychology within the legal system to create safer communities and to assist people to find pathways away from criminal behaviour.'[8]

At a risk of sounding like 'sour grapes' (that is, mine), the current situation may leave some psychologists that work routinely with police without the title of forensic psychologist, and now probably better described more generally as 'psychologists who work with police'. Although the work they (and I) do is often very much still within the realms of forensic psychology, it is often more than offender rehabilitation or helping police to better understand criminals and their behaviour; for example, helping police to make better decisions in criminal investigations or how to communicate better in appeals to the public for information on specific crimes. Unsurprisingly perhaps, this covers many of the topics in this book. If the reader was expecting a chapter on the rehabilitation of offenders, then they are advised, metaphorically at least, to call a taxi now and avoid disappointment. So what do psychologists do with police?

It is not uncommon for psychologists who engage with police work, for example, to be asked to assist in trying to determine whether a series of crimes should be attributed to the same offender, or instead to multiple (that is, different offenders). In the absence of forensic evidence or any reliable accounts by eye-witnesses, in an approach commonly referred to as 'crime linking', some will analyse a potential series of crimes for 'behavioural consistency' (for example, whether and how an offender speaks to his/her victims) with high behavioural consistency taken as being more indicative of the same offender being present, than where low behavioural consistency is found.[9] In terms of police investigations, such a distinction is vitally important for criminal investigators and the investigative decisions that they have to make; for example, whether to divide limited (finite) investigative resources to look for several different (independent) offenders, or to concentrate resources on looking for just one, in terms of concentrating resources on house-to-house enquiries, this distinction can guide whether this is spread evenly over several different areas of a town or city, or whether they are concentrated on looking for evidence in just one area. We now expand on this example to look at one of the best-known interfaces between psychologists and policing. Enter *offender profiling.*

Offender profiling

Offender profiling comprises a series of different techniques sometimes employed in criminal investigations to help identify unknown serious offenders for specific (often serial) offences. In the last century, films such as 'Silence of the Lambs', television drama series, such as 'Cracker' ('Fitz' in the US version), and crime fiction novels, such as *Wire in the Blood*, have portrayed psychologists as mystical beings with the power to read the minds of others (that is, criminals) from the crime scenes that they leave behind. Possessing powers of insight that only a few 'gifted' people are blessed with. Time and time again the investigative utility of their 'profiles' is seemingly demonstrated, whereby they provide valuable clues and evidence which police use to finally identify serious criminals (often serial murderers) after what have been to that point seemingly fruitless investigations (Roach and Selby-Fell, forthcoming). In the US, such a perception of psychologists as offender profilers has been propagated by autobiographical accounts by ex-Federal Bureau of Investigation (FBI) agents, such as Robert Ressler, and in the UK similar accounts of 'profiler contributions' to serious crime investigations have been provided by psychologists including David Canter and Paul Britton.[10] A detailed examination of the utility of offender profiling has been expertly provided by numerous academics over the past three decades (for example, see Canter, 1994; Ainsworth, 2001; Alison, 2005) so is not presented here.

Offender profiling is, however, not a homogenous approach as it comprises different psychological (and non-psychological) methods and techniques employed to assist with the identification of serious, as yet unidentified, (and often serial) offenders. The original method, for example, was first developed in the US by the FBI (for example, see Ressler et al, 1986) but other methods have been developed by psychiatrists, clinical psychologists, personality psychologists, and psycho-geographers (see Ainsworth, 2001, for an excellent account).

Regardless of the preferred approach, offender profiling relies on a series of common assumptions. What is important is not the detail of the differing profiling techniques and methods, but what they generally have in common: (i) behavioural consistency and (ii) offender homology (Alison et al, 2007; Woodhams et al, 2007).

Taking the first assumption, for one to consider the profiling of an unknown offender from the crime scene they leave behind, to be actually feasible, the individual's behaviour must remain sufficiently consistent across their crimes (for example, if he/she talks to his/her victims while sexually assaulting them then he/she should do this with each consecutive victim (Woodhams et al, 2007). There is some evidence to support this from research on rape and burglary (for example, Alison et al, 2007) and serial murder (for example, Salfati and Bateman, 2005; Woodhams et al, 2007). That said, Woodhams et al (2007) concluded that linking offences to offenders by behavioural analysis was fraught with difficulties, with none greater than the unreliability of offender behavioural consistency.

Taking the second assumption, Mokros and Alison describe it as the 'homology assumption': 'The same behavioural dispositions that determine the style of the crime scene behaviour are reflected in more general, non-offense patterns in the individual's life' (Mokros and Alison, 2002, p 118).

Put more simply, the offender homology assumes that where two different offenders are of the same 'personality type' they will commit a crime in the same way (Alison et al, 2007) and that the way a serious offender commits their crimes will be suitably different from the ways that others do. The original FBI profiling approach, for example, maintains that if two crime scenes are the same then the same type of individual committed them: an 'organised' or a 'disorganised' personality. It suffices to say for the needs of this book, that such evidence for offender homology is hotly contested (for example, see Mokros and Alison, 2002).

With the fragility (and some say contentiousness) of the first and second assumptions of offender profiling now briefly highlighted, then it will come as no surprise to the reader that that offender profiling is not seen as being vital to contemporary criminal investigations as it was or is still in fictional representations of criminal investigations, at least in the UK anyway. Indeed, any 'heyday' for police use of offender profiling, in the UK at least, lasted little more than a decade (the 1990s) as advances in forensic science and other new investigative tools became available and were added to the police armoury (for example, mobile/cell phone data and social media footprints), to help police investigators identify serious criminals more quickly, and arguably more accurately, reducing the demand for the services of offender profilers, many of whom were psychologists. That said, just to confuse further, there are still a few working with the UK National Crime Agency, but they do not refer to themselves as profilers.

In terms of charting an evolution of the relationship between psychology and crime, is it fair to say that offender (psychological) profiling was a key point in the relationship between psychologists and police. As Peter Ainsworth summarised back in 2001, 'Offender (or psychological) profiling provides perhaps one of the best examples of the way in which psychology can be applied to police work' (Ainsworth, 2001, p 142).

Although Peter Ainsworth's statement was no doubt a fair appraisal in 2001, what has been less so is how offender profiling has been presented by the media, particularly in the 1980s and 1990s, whereby it was arguably the most depicted and popularised area of psychology, especially where the services of 'mystical psychologists' were employed by police. In the past decade, as the interest of the media in offender profiling/profilers has remained strong (perhaps demonstrated by the never-ending drama series (especially from Scandinavia) and by popular crime fiction novels, any initial enthusiasm shown by UK policing for employing the services of offender profilers has waned due to increased reliance on forensic science, social media analysis, and mobile phone analysis, in criminal investigations. Nevertheless, for better or worse, offender profiling should be considered as an important stage in charting the history of the relationship between psychology and policing.

We now move to another area/aspect of policing where psychological research, knowledge, and theory has, and continues to make, a significant contribution to policing: *interviewing suspects and witnesses*. We begin this section, however, with a brief foray into the psychology of deception as preparation for Chapter 6 which suggests how some psychology can be used to detect liars on the street.

Detecting lies and deception

Granhag et al (2014) describe deception as a false depiction of words or conduct of matter of fact or law, made intentionally to convince someone that something is true but which the liar believes is untrue. In order for a human being to deceive others there is an essential 'psychological/cognitive ingredient', for human beings to be able to deceive each other. This is known as *Theory of Mind* (ToM) and is presented in Box 2.3.

An area of policing where psychology can and continues to make an important contribution is in helping to detect deception, particularly that exercised in police-suspect interview scenarios. Interestingly, psychological research in this area has identified two common misperceptions about the detection of deception (particularly lying) which has major implications for

Box 2.3: Theory of Mind: the essential ingredient in deception

Theory of Mind (ToM) is probably the best known of all human social cognition mechanisms (Roach and Pease, 2013). It is the capacity for a person to have a 'testable belief' (a theory) about the content of another person's mind. Although this sounds all a bit 'science fiction', it is simply the ability to know that others can have different thoughts and feelings (that is, mental states) which can drive their behaviour. More importantly, we can appreciate that, at any one time, the actual content of these mental states can differ from our own. In short, we know that they can have different thoughts and feelings to our own.

How do you get a ToM in the first place? Psychologists have identified that most children will begin to develop a ToM between two and four years, which probably accounts for the notorious 'terrible twos', when most children begin to realise that others have different thoughts and wants to them, and more importantly that what they think and want is not necessarily shared by others! This is usually reinforced by adults beginning to use the word 'no', and boy do toddlers not like that!

So, what has this got to do with deception and the deceiving of others? Quite simply everything. If you do not know that others have different thoughts and feelings to you then how can you trick them, as you will think they think exactly what you think and so will know your intentions!

A world full of humans without ToM might appear at face-value to have some benefits, with for example no lies and no fraud, but this would be a cold, callous world without love, empathy, humour, and friendship and thanks to ToM us humans have evolved to be one of the most sociable of species. That said, it still bestows us with the ability to deceive, to lie, and to cheat when we want to. Especially when we try to cover up our involvement in crime!

police interviewers, particularly as an overwhelming amount of research has consistently shown that us humans are not as good at spotting lies as we think we are (for example, see Vrij and Semin, 1996; Vrij, 2008, 2014). Primarily, this is likely to be because we tend to hold inaccurate beliefs about non-verbal and verbal cues to liars and lying. For example, most of us will be taught as children that lying is bad, so the misconception follows that someone lying will behave differently to someone telling the truth, largely due to the 'psychological effects' of lying. Box 2.4 presents two psychological approaches to identifying non-verbal *Deception-Leakage Theory* (Colls et al, 2001) and *Four Factor Theory* (Zuckerman, De Paulo, and Rosenthal, 1981; Zuckerman and Driver, 1985).

Research evidence to date suggests strongly that police often use common, yet unreliable, human 'subjective deception cues'; often behaviours

---

Box 2.4: Detecting deception: Leakage and the Four Factor Theory

Leakage Theory is where non-verbal behaviours are believed to be a form of communication that are powerful and pervasive (Vrij, 2008). For example, if an individual attempted to cause deception, they might display observable psychological or behavioural changes, such as tapping their fingers on a desk or rocking on their chair. Leakages are often considered to be indicators of deception by police officers (Nortje & Tredoux, 2019; Colls et al, 2001).

That said, many of the subjective indicators that we typically use to judge whether someone is telling the truth or not, have been proved unreliable (for example, suspect avoids eye-contact) mainly because changes in psychological state are not always due to deception, but other factors such as fear or anxiety (Nortje & Tredoux, 2019). Aldert Vrij (2008), one of the principal psychologists researching this area, reports that such *Subjective Deception Cues* are things people believe to be indicators of lying, but which might not actually be.

The **Four Factor Theory** (for example, see Zuckerman et al,1981; Zuckerman and Driver, 1985; De Paulo et al, 2003) also uses subjective deception cues, whereby deception is associated with four psychological factors.

1. *Emotion* – deceivers often exhibit emotional responses as a direct result of feelings of guilt and/or fear of detection (Granhag et al, 2014). Ekman (1988) states that the fear of getting caught to be greatest when the risk of punishment is known to the individual.
2. *Physiological arousal* – based on an increase in psychological arousal identified by the Polygraph Test (see Box 2.3) such as increased blood pressure (Granhag et al, 2014). Kahneman (1973), however, states that an individual is likely to experiences greater levels of arousal when they are faced with a complex, unusual, or threatening situation, and not just when deceiving.
3. Deception as *cognitively demanding* as liars have to formulate a lie and ensure that they are consistent with the external information (Granhag et al, 2014). Vrij et al (2009) argue that the formation of a lie puts an observable strain on the person lying.
4. *Behavioural control* – people who are believed to be deceiving often attempt to behave in a manner which showcases them as honest. Resulting in their behaviour appearing rehearsed (Granhag et al, 2014).

---

associated include 'nervousness' (for example, Delmas et al, 2019) which is what most people feel when being interviewed in any situation whether guilty or otherwise! In a meta-analysis of research findings conducted by DePaulo et al (2003), it was concluded that to focus on non-verbal behaviour cues is generally of less efficacy (that is, accuracy) than focusing on verbal cues. We now turn to psychological approaches to detecting verbal deception; that is, lying liars and truthful truth tellers, in police-suspect and witness interviews.

Interviewing suspects and witnesses

In the UK up until the mid-1980s, most convictions for serious crimes were secured by confession, many of which were later found to be at best, suspicious, and at worst, false. Indeed, an unforgivable percentage of confessions were likely to have been secured under duress while the suspect was being 'interviewed'. The Police and Criminal Evidence Act (PACE) (1984) was introduced in England and Wales primarily to counter the growing feeling that the UK public was beginning to lose confidence in its police and criminal justice system. Mainly to both better balance the rights of the individual and the powers of the police and by making police practice more consistent across all UK police forces.[11] Importantly, this included the interviewing of suspects.

Interviewing police suspects

A review of police training at the time of PACE (1984) identified existing police interview techniques to be often wholly inappropriate and generally inadequate, and therefore an area where psychological research could be employed to help to improve investigator skills.

Psychologists, such as professors Ray Bull and Becky Milne, have spent decades conducting research in support of police interviewers and to inform the development of 'investigative interviewing', including the PEACE training package which is a five-step process within which to structure interviews in criminal investigations (**P**lanning and preparation; **E**ngage and explain; **A**ccount; **C**losure; **E**valuation).[12]

It suffices here to simply state that another major point of interaction between psychological research and policing has been in the development of the interviewing of police suspects. For example, the reader is directed to explore the numerous reviews of different 'psychologically based tools' for helping detect lies and deceit, including the *Guilty Knowledge Test* (used in conjunction with the *Polygraph Test* or lie-detector), the *Statement Validity Test*, and *Reality Monitoring* (for example, see Vrij, 2008 for an excellent account not provided here).

Curiously, the contribution of psychological research in police interviewing of witnesses to crimes remains less of a focus and is briefly explored in the next section.

Interviewing police witnesses

Research conducted over the past few decades by psychologists has seen the development of new ways of assisting witnesses to recall as much as information as possible about the crimes that they have witnessed (Roach and Selby-Fell, forthcoming). One such technique, known as the 'cognitive interview' (CI) (Geiselman et al, 1985) utilises theories from cognitive psychology (for example, how human memory works) and social psychology (for example, how to build rapport and good communication skills) to help witnesses to re-instate key aspects of the context of the crime in their minds, and to 'trigger' other aspects which hitherto might not have been retrieved (Roach and Selby-Fell, forthcoming). Building rapport with an interviewee as a means of obtaining reliable information from interviews has a rich history and the reader is directed to the work of Laurence Alison et al, particularly *Rapport: The Four Ways to Read People* by Emily and Laurence Alison (2020), for a great demonstration of the importance of 'rapport building' in police interview scenarios.

CIs are commonly used in the UK and are a form of memory retrieval and consist of an assortment of communication techniques with which to better obtain a greater amount of information from interviewees, and generally comprise four key features (for example, see Geiselman, Fisher, MacKinnon, and Holland, 1985; Memon, Meissner, and Fraser, 2010):

1. Witnesses are told to report everything, including information they may think of as being not vital.
2. Next, they are asked to think back to the physical context mentally and recall what was happening and how they were feeling.
3. Next, they are advised to recall the same events but in a different order (Adler & Gray, 2010). In doing so, this can increase observable deception cues and observer accuracy in judging veracity (lying and truth-telling). This can create behavioural differences between people who are telling the truth and those causing deception (Masip et al, 2016). However, if a person rehearses the events in a reversed chronological order, they may well be proficient at this making it difficult to spot the difference between deceivers and truth tellers (Leins et al, 2013).
4. Finally, interviewees are asked to recall events from the perspective of someone else (not them) at the scene (Adler & Gray, 2010).

One major advantage of the cognitive interview approach identified by researchers is that interviewers can use it to decrease fear and arousal in interviewees so that they feel more comfortable (for example, established by rapport building). Only then can they best share what they can remember. Several practical implications have been found, however, with regard conducting CIs, including variations in cognitive skills according to an interviewee's gender, socio-economic group, and ethnicity (Vogl and Vogl, 2015).

Interestingly, in a majority of the psychological research to date, police have been found to perform no better (or only marginally better) than non-police participants in lie/truth-detection studies (for example, Yarbrough, 2020).

Psychology and police decision-making

In terms of research in this area, and for some unfathomable reason, psychology came rather late to the party. That said, police decision-making has increasingly become an important focus for psychologists and continues to be used to inform UK police practice, particularly regarding training. This research comes from two directions: top-down, for example, whereby knowledge obtained from *traditional* psychological research and experimentation in a non-police setting is imported and applied in a policing context. The experimental work of Daniel Kahneman and Amos Tversky (for example, see Kahneman, Slovic, and Tversky, 1982, discussed in the next chapter) on human decision-making and cognition has seen many of the findings applied to policing contexts, especially regarding their system one and system two processes and the influence of cognitive bias (Rossmo, 2009; Kahneman, 2011). The other direction is a more 'ground-up' *naturalistic* research approach, whereby police are observed making decisions in real-world encounters, such as what might make them suspicious of someone when out on patrol. Both directions have begun to contribute significantly to the understanding and enhancement of police decision-making in a plethora of different police contexts and situations, such as police decision-making in time-poor, split-second contexts, such as whether to shoot a suspect who is endangering the lives of others (for example, Roycroft and Roach, 2019).

Identifying common psychological (cognitive) bias such as tunnel-vision, confirmation bias, and heuristics (mental short-cuts) (see Kahneman, 2011) has become important for identifying how unconscious and conscious bias can have a negative influence on the decision-making and conduct of police, particularly in criminal investigations. As psychological research and its importance to areas of policing is presented in more detail in Chapter 3, it suffices to provide a short introduction here.

Psychological research has identified how police, as human beings, can make biased decisions such as assumptions about victims (for example, what are referred to as common 'rape myths' – covered in Chapter 3) when investigating sexual offences; for example, if a victim/survivor does not fit the common stereotype, evidence suggests that some police will not believe them as they do not feel that they appear to look, present, or sound like they believe a genuine victim would or should.

Furthermore, the negative effects of different types of cognitive bias leading to 'investigative failure' (Rossmo, 2009) has been identified by psychologists; for example, when investigators move too prematurely from the identification of a prime suspect to the building of an evidential case against a suspect, exemplified in the late 1970s where a 'hoaxer' was believed erroneously by police investigators to be the actual 'Yorkshire Ripper', a serial murderer of at least 13 women (see, for example, Roach and Pease, 2016).

Psychological research in this area has therefore made, and continues to make, a positive contribution to police decision-making, particularly regarding minimising 'investigative failure' (Rossmo, 2009), as shall be shown in the next chapter.

Psychology and the prevention of crime

Another area of policing which has proved popular with psychological research has been in the 'prevention of crime'. Traditionally perhaps, crime prevention has been perceived as simply making things harder to steal (that is, 'target hardening') (Clarke, 1980, 1997); for example, fitting sturdy locks, bolts, and alarms to make it more difficult to steal something, such as the theft of a motor vehicle or committing burglary. Over the past 30 years or so, this simplistic view of preventing crime has given way to a plethora of psychological and criminological research aimed at influencing decision-making, not just of likely offenders, but also that of the potential victims of crime (that is, all of us). In UK policing it is common for psychologists to advise or help police to reduce specific crime problems in 'hot-spot' areas (for example, see Ratcliffe, 2009, 2016); for example, reducing student burglary victimisation by raising awareness of their lack of security-conscious behaviour (for example, Roach et al, 2018), such as forgetting to lock their doors and windows when going out.

The contribution of psychological knowledge and research to crime prevention will be explored in greater detail in Chapter 7.

Chapter summary

This chapter has hopefully provided the reader with some idea of the historical relationship between crime, policing, craft, science, and psychology. Although not an exhaustive list, some key points where psychological research has interacted with, and indeed influenced, aspects of policing, including offender profiling, the interviewing of suspects and witnesses, and crime prevention, have been highlighted to demonstrate how psychological research can improve police practice.

With the introductions now complete, the remainder of this book will provide more depth of discussion in key areas where psychology and policing can and should be more than simply 'welcome bedfellows' and become enthusiastic partners.

Further reading

Ainsworth, P. (2001) *Psychology and Policing*, Cullompton, Devon: Willan.

Ratcliffe, J.H. (2016) *Intelligence-Led Policing* (2nd edn), London: Routledge.

Rossmo, D.K. (ed) (2009) *Criminal Investigative Failures*, Boca Raton: CRC Press.

Sherman, L.W. (1998) *Evidence-Based Policing*, Washington, DC: Police Foundation.

Vrij, A. (2008) *Detecting Lies and Deceit: Pitfalls and Opportunities* (2nd edn), Chichester: John Wiley & Sons.

Wortley, R., Sidebottom, A., Tilley, N., and Laycock, G. (eds) (2019) *Routledge Handbook of Crime Science*, Abingdon, Oxford: Routledge.

Suggested resources

UCL Jill Dando Institute for Security and Crime Science: https://www.ucl.ac.uk/jill-dando-institute/

Society of Evidence-Based Policing: https://www.sebp.police.uk/

3

Human and police decision-making

Introduction

In the hope of achieving a seamless continuation from the previous chapter, we move next to look at what is arguably the most obvious arena in which psychology and policing interact – *police 'decision-making'*. We begin with a brief introduction to the psychology of human decision-making ('RoboCop' aside, those working in policing are humans after all),[1] before looking at a common model adopted by UK and US police at least, to better understand and deal with the underlying mechanisms involved with a crime – the 'problem-solving approach', in this case the SARA model (see Box 3.2).

We will, albeit briefly, look at some of the guidance and training currently available to UK police to aid them with making decisions, including the National Decision Model (NDM) developed by the UK College of Policing[2] before expanding to explore the psychology of human bias and error, with particular focus on police decision-making in criminal investigations, often referred to as *investigative decision-making.* Cases of homicide and sexual offences have more recently become a burgeoning area for psychological research and its interaction with policing.

Policing is often an incredibly difficult profession in which effective decisions (in sheer volume and magnitude if nothing else) need to be made in double-quick time. This chapter concludes with some well-meant suggestions as to how good police and investigative decision-making can be enhanced, while at the same time, how negative influences that promote 'bad' and erroneous police decision-making can be reduced.

The fact that police are 'human beings' (a point sometimes lost by some in the media) means that they rely on the same brains and cognitive processes that the rest of us do. This accepted, then an appropriate starting point is to explore human decision-making processes in general, before moving to how these processes are used by those involved in policing. There is an argument to be made that not enough of this more general 'human species-wide' research has been imported (for example, from experiments in laboratories) into the policing world, or that indeed not enough research on decision-making has focused on police and policing. We begin more generally perhaps with human decision-making.

Human decision-making

How we humans make decisions is influenced by a large number of different factors, including: the context and situation, our personality, our previous experiences, our levels of knowledge, to name but few. Evolutionary processes have provided us with incredibly powerful brains capable of not just instant decision-making, referred to as *system one thinking* or more commonly, as 'intuition' (see, for example, Kahneman, 2011), but we are also able to put the cognitive 'brakes' on our thinking, by employing a more conscious and deliberate process known as *system two thinking* (Kahneman, 2011). System two is therefore the more rational, calculating, 'risk–reward weigher-upper' way of thinking, but as we shall see, it cannot not guarantee against us still making bad or sometimes catastrophic decisions, even if we actively choose to employ it. For infallibility, we definitely need to look beyond ourselves and also probably also well beyond the planet we inhabit too!

System one thinking is to some degree shared with most of the animal kingdom whereby survival often depends on reacting quickly to danger in order to live and, quite literally, to fight another day (Roach and Pease, 2013). If you bring to mind any wildlife documentary that you have seen in the past, I bet that virtually every animal or organism shown in any episode will have had to wrestle with the twin challenges of getting food and while avoiding becoming something else's dinner. Slow decision-making in such hunter–prey scenarios is not usually a recipe for longevity but the exact opposite; hence; much of our instinctual decision-making is cognisant of 'fight or flight' fame. Although a vast majority of humans do not have any natural predators left these days to worry about as such, the older parts of our brain architecture are still the same as that of our 'lion avoiding' forebears (Roach and Pease, 2013). Of course, lions for most of us nowadays (lion-tamers and zookeepers aside) are way down the list of daily risks that we are exposed to, and we are at more danger from our fellow humans or our 'conspecifics', as war and crimes of violence sadly all too frequently are testimony.[3]

In some respects, life was simpler and less hazardous when our species was more worried more about the threat of lions. Although, on a more optimistic note, eminent psychologist Professor Stephen Pinker has recently suggested that there is less violence in the world than at any point in history (Pinker, 2011). Presumably this reduction in violence is not all down to a reduction in the frequency of lions as a common danger to humans or more zoos would be needed not prisons!

As we shall see when we look at cognitive bias in decision-making, this quick system one thinking serves us well in many different decision-making contexts where time is at a premium, but it can also be our downfall in others.

One of the most significant ways in which we humans can be distinguished from most other living organisms is our ability to engage in deeper levels of

Box 3.1: Is committing crime a product of rational or irrational decision-making?

Crime is generally considered to be rational behaviour (at least in the short term) if the criminal employs reason and 'acts purposely to gain desired ends' (Walsh and Ellis, 2007, p 56). Cornish and Clarke's (1986, 2006, 2008) rational choice perspective is centred in the here-and-now of offender choice-making and is concerned with the influence of a current environment on the decision-making and behaviour of those who are faced with an opportunity to commit a crime, such as spotting a handbag in an unattended vehicle with the rear window open.

The significance of Rational Choice Theory when applied to crime is that it predicts that individuals will offend if they consider the environment and situation conducive to do so; that is, if the perceived risks are sufficiently low and perceived rewards sufficiently high. The perception of risk and reward is obviously subjective.

We explore further how this interpretation of criminal decision-making is adopted by Situational Crime Prevention (Chapter 7).

thinking that transport us way beyond a reliance on reflexive and instinctual reactions, such as running for cover. As mentioned in the previous chapter, sometimes referred to as 'rational thought', system two thinking (for example, Kahneman, 2011) gives us a deeper decision-making process option; for example, when you are deciding on whether to become a police officer or to take a less hazardous career route and become an academic researcher.[4] An ability to deliberate and weigh up the options available to us does not, of course, make us immune to committing errors, anymore than it protects us from occasionally making seemingly ridiculous decisions, especially when all the options available to us are bad and we strive to choose the 'least worst' one. But it does arguably offer us the chance of making the most likely to be correct decision (rather than always 'shooting from the hip') and help us to salve our consciences, if need be, by allowing us to justify making what turned out to be an error, by claiming that we have at least 'given it some thought'. 'It' being whatever it was that we made a wrong decision about. As Guy Bellamy (1982) in *The Sinners Congregation* suggests, 'hindsight is an exact science'. Might I suggest that it is the only one too, often leading to embarrassment by illuminating our mistakes and errors brighter than the brightest star in the night sky. So please don't be so hard on yourselves (and others) for being human. As Mr D used to say to those of us in his English class, 'engage your brains before speaking', which looking back now appears to be a euphemism for 'use your system two thinking Roach, before you ask another daft question'. Yet another example of the vision of this great teacher.[5]

Making decisions 'rationally' and making rational decisions

Next, we turn our focus from general humans to those of us humans who commit crimes and break rules; that is, offender decision-making – a far more popular spotlight for criminologists. Although this is explored more fully in Chapter 7, Box 3.1 presents why some see committing crime as a rational choice.

Decision-making in the real world (or how to act less like a robot)

One interesting alternative explanation for how we make decisions which questions the 'rational choice' assumption is Daniel Kahneman and Amos Tversky's (1979) *Prospect Theory.* Essentially, Prospect Theory presents a behavioural model which explains how we decide between alternative choices which involve risk and uncertainty, including how we 'weigh up' the likelihood of success and failure and of gains and losses (Kahneman & Tversky, 1979; Kahneman, 2011). The point of departure from the sometimes rather crude rational choice approach (for example, commit the crime or don't commit the crime?) is that Prospect Theory suggests that we tend to make decisions in terms of 'expected utility' (that is, what we will get) in relation to a reference point, like taking in to account how much money we currently have, rather than simply what we might get if we win (or absolute outcomes). Re-stated slightly differently, we may feel more or less inclined to take a risk depending on how we are feeling and what our situation at the time; for example, we may be less likely to steal from a shop if we are happy that we have just been paid.

In other words, we tend to generally favour decisions where we are more certain to get some reward or utility, over those where we might get a big reward but are at a high risk of getting nothing additional and losing what we had in the first place. This is known as the certainty/possibility effect (Kahneman and Tversky, 1979). Thinking about it, if forced to do so, then those of us who are not of a 'gambling nature' will be more likely to bet on a horse considered to be the 'favourite' to win and receive some return (however small) and minimise our losses if it wins, than put a large bet on a rank-outsider even though if it wins we will receive a much bigger pay-out. Favourites in horse racing (or any other sports) are called so for good reason, primarily because bookmakers expect them to win; for example, because they have won numerous previous races, they have a top jockey riding them, or they like the good-to-firm ground. If, however, we have recently won a sizeable fortune on the UK National Lottery and are spending a day at the races merely for personal enjoyment, then we may be more tempted to put a significant bet on an outsider, as losing will not seem as devastating because we still have our rather large pile of cash back at home! Prospect Theory, therefore, considers the context and emotional state we are in, when trying to understand how people make decisions.[6]

Prospect Theory was developed from experimental research using the framing of different risky choices, and consistently the finding was that people tend to be loss-averse; that is, we dislike losses more than equivalent gains. Indeed, the findings suggest that we are more willing to take risks to avoid a loss than to achieve a gain (Kahneman and Tversky, 1979). This will be explored further in Chapter 7 where research looking at theft from insecure vehicles using the *Nudge* (Thaler and Sunstein, 2008) approach is presented.

So, what are the implications for understanding the decision to commit a crime? The point is simple – that those thinking of committing a crime are not likely to simply weigh up the risks and rewards of doing so in a cold and calculating, robot-like way, and then act or not act accordingly (as Rational Choice Theory in its purest interpretation might have us believe). Barbed wire may put most of us off but for others it is simply an 'occupational hazard' and not a deterrent; for example, they might have wire-cutters in the boot of their car. We return to this point when we explore the relationship between psychology research and crime prevention in Chapter 6.

The reader may be forgiven for feeling that to up this point that I have painted a rather simplistic picture of human decision-making and that there are many factors and contexts that can (and do) influence a decision to commit a crime (or not). Or simply, what has all this got to do with police decision-making? That said, there is human decision-making research that we can work with which identifies common ways in which we all make decisions, but I acknowledge the point that understanding how decision-making occurs is highly complex and far from an exact science, perhaps exemplified no better than when attempting to study decision-making by those in an occupation as complex as policing (Roycroft and Roach, 2019). Compare extant research literature focusing on offender/criminal decision-making and you will quickly see that by volume it swamps that focused on police decision-making. Although, more detail on how police make decisions is arguably for another day (or book, should I be allowed to write another), the remainder of this chapter should at least be seen as shedding light on what hopefully continues to be an emerging relationship between psychology research and policing. So, what do we know about police decision-making?

Police as decision-makers

'Police officers attempt to make sense of the circumstances that confront them, respond to developments and take control by making decisions using the most powerful and adept tool available to them: their brains' (Bryant, 2018, p 48).

In an article published in 2013 on the website of the *Guardian* newspaper, the writer suggested that although many jobs and roles are predicted to become obsolete in the next two decades due to 'automation' (for example, workers in fast-food restaurants and tax collectors), those less likely to disappear will be those which require the building of complex relationships with clients and the public, such as nursing and policing.[7] With the threat of 'Robocop' seemingly fictional, at least for the foreseeable future, then a greater understanding of how police make decisions and how they might be better supported to do so, remains of high importance, with psychological research being a major player driving forward.

Decision-making by police is commonly situated within a unique blend of legal, moral, and procedural demands, mixed with a plethora of different community expectations and available resources (Roycroft and Roach, 2019). Take the first officer present at a potential assault – she/he must decide almost simultaneously, if life needs to be preserved and, if so, inform the other emergency services how best to protect evidence that could lead potentially to a conviction for a crime, and who are likely to be needed as witnesses? Later in the same shift, they may be called to attend a suspected arson, before then helping to defuse a violent situation between spouses, before ending their shift by dealing with a reported break-in at a local school. The modern police officer has a multitude of different concerns to deal with, many at the same time, before they can make any operationally focused decisions. Whether, for example, to administer a breath test to an 85-year-old driver of a vehicle travelling at 33 miles per hour in a maximum 30 miles per hour zone, and who appears upset about being stopped. Thoughts going through an officer's mind are likely to include are they upset because they are otherwise law-abiding and are unaccustomed to being stopped by police? Are they not upset but angry about being stopped? Do they have something to hide? Lots of decision-making needs to occur and in a very short space of time. Robin Bryant sums it up brilliantly: 'What is perhaps surprising is not just that many, but probably most decisions in policing demand reasoning in circumstances which are novel (often unique) and unfamiliar. This is particularly the case with the critical incident' (Bryant, 2018, p 64). Put simply, every police officer the world over and irrespective of rank or role has to make an abundance of decisions on a daily basis. Many will be minor, routine, and seemingly inconsequential, but some will be potentially life changing (or lifesaving) for an officer, a member of the public, or both. Unfortunately, sometimes seemingly trivial and routine decision-making can indeed become more serious than is first anticipated, highlighted only by the luxury of hindsight. For example, it is tragically all too common for US police officers who stop people for minor driving offences to be confronted by a serious criminal-driver with a gun. Police decision-making in such circumstances can quite literally mean life or death (Roach and Pease, 2016).

Again, psychology can play a part in helping police to make decisions in often-dangerous circumstances (covered in later chapters).

We begin our exploration of police decision-making in less dramatic fashion, with a brief look at police decision-making and problem-solving.

Crime as a problem to be solved

For the last half-century or so, there has been a gradual shift in police thinking away from the traditional approach of simply 'reacting to a crime' after it has happened; for example, from just identifying those who commit it (which admittedly is a form of crime prevention provided you get the right man or woman) to thinking about how to prevent it happening in the first place. Arguably, the most noticeable difference in police thinking has been a move away from viewing crime prevention as simply being about making places, things, and people more physically secure (for example, fitting alarms and immobilisers to cars to deter would-be car thieves) to instead focus on better understanding of the underlying causes and mechanisms behind a specific crime problem (for example, which cars are targeted most, how, where, when, and why?) *Problem-Orientated Policing* (POP) embodies this approach (for example, Goldstein, 1977, 2018; Goldstein and Susmilch, 1982).

As was briefly touched upon in Chapter 2, the late great Herman Goldstein developed a problem-solving approach to understanding and responding effectively to crime and policing problems:

> Problem-oriented policing is an approach to policing in which discrete pieces of police business (each consisting of a cluster of similar incidents, whether crime or acts of disorder, that the police are expected to handle) are subject to microscopic examination (drawing on the especially honed skills of crime analysts and the accumulated experience of operating field personnel) in hopes that what is freshly learned about each problem will lead to discovering a new and more effective strategy for dealing with it. [8]

For the past three decades the SARA problem-solving model (see Box 3.2) has proved popular with police around the world, particularly in the UK and US. Essentially, SARA is a model to help police better understand and so respond more effectively to crime and policing problems – first, by identifying a specific crime problem in need of preventing (scanning); second, by understanding what is causing and sustaining that problem (analysis); third, by exploring the most appropriate means by which that problem can be tackled (response); and fourth, by evaluating the degree to which the response has been effective at reducing that crime problem (assessment). A more detailed account of the SARA model is presented in Box 3.2.

Box 3.2: The SARA problem-solving model

The SARA model contains the following elements.[9]

Scanning:

- Identifying recurring problems of concern to the public and the police.
- Identifying the consequences of the problem for the community and the police.
- Prioritising those problems.
- Developing broad goals.
- Confirming that the problems exist.
- Determining how frequently the problem occurs and how long it has been taking place.
- Selecting problems for closer examination.

Analysis:

- Identifying and understanding the events and conditions that precede and accompany the problem.
- Identifying relevant data to be collected.
- Researching what is known about the problem type.
- Taking inventory of how the problem is currently addressed and the strengths and limitations of the current response.
- Narrowing the scope of the problem as specifically as possible.
- Identifying a variety of resources that may be of assistance in developing a deeper understanding of the problem.
- Developing a working hypothesis about why the problem is occurring.

Response:

- Brainstorming for new interventions.
- Searching for what other communities with similar problems have done.
- Choosing among the alternative interventions.
- Outlining a response plan and identifying responsible parties.
- Stating the specific objectives for the response plan.
- Carrying out the planned activities.

Assessment:

- Determining whether the plan was implemented (a process evaluation).
- Collecting pre- and post-response qualitative and quantitative data.
- Determining whether broad goals and specific objectives were attained.
- Identifying any new strategies needed to augment the original plan.
- Conducting ongoing assessment to ensure continued effectiveness.

Problem-Orientated Policing (POP) with its emphasis on understanding a specific crime problem to select the most successful way it might be addressed, might nowadays sound like 'stating the obvious', but up until Herman Goldstein's seminal work on problem-solving in policing, whether crime prevention interventions worked or not was much more of a hit 'n' miss affair. By way of example, about 20 years ago, when I was a mere slip of a lad and new to researching in the crime and policing field, I began looking at how to reduce the number of thefts from sheds in a particular part of a particular town, in a particular part of England.[10] Although admittedly this was not the most serious or heinous of crimes (or for that matter the serial murder investigations which I believed I would be more qualified to assist with at the time), those having their sheds broken into were understandably angry about it and wanted the police to make it stop. Hell-bent on taking a 'problem-orientated policing' approach to this tricky problem, I set about trying to find as much information about said 'shed-thefts' as possible, before devising my 'brilliant' interventions which I believed would stand more chance of being successful than anything previously known ever to woman or man.[11] Before sharing my thoughts with the fantastic police sergeant (who had been unfortunate enough to have been given me as his charge in the last month of his otherwise relatively idiot-free, 35-year policing career) I asked him what he would do ordinarily to solve this kind of problem. After pausing for what felt like about two days, he said, "I'd get a leaflet put through every letterbox of every front-door in this area, telling them to put a big padlock on their shed-doors and to store their gardening equipment and bikes elsewhere." Sensing a little sarcasm, I asked whether he had any evidence that this 'leafleting approach' that he had used in past had worked and so had reduced the number of reported thefts form sheds? Again, he took what felt about two days to reply, before saying:

> 'I don't know to be honest as I've never checked. There was a mix-up with the printing firm and they accidentally supplied us with over 20,000 of the things which are taking up most of the space in that large cupboard behind you. My inspector wants the space to store our new radio comms equipment, so leafleting to prevent thefts from sheds is a no-brainer for me.'

In the short space of time that we worked together, I learnt a lot of brilliant things from this wonderful policeman, but alas how to adopt a POP approach to crime was sadly not one of them.

If the volume of background noise in which police must make decisions is often great (including over-ordering the number of leaflets at a printers), how can we help police to make more effective and evidence-based decisions?

Let us take a brief look at the guidance and training available to UK police regarding how they should make decisions.

The Police National Decision Model

'Some circumstances in policing are common, familiar and although sometimes complicated are not usually unduly complex and remain largely predictable. Decisions in these settings are likely to be rule-based ("Standard Operating Procedures"), with little need to deviate from what was learned during training' (Bryant, 2018, p 63).

As Bryant goes on to suggest, the problem is that these types of decisions will almost certainly constitute the minority that police have to make, a point we return to later in the chapter.

There is, of course, no known system of decision-making that can guarantee infallibility in policing or otherwise. Taking a decision often necessitates taking risks even when we reason to the most likely outcome (Bryant, 2018). Of course, to avoid all does not ensure success. Police decision-making is often a complex set of interrelated decisions, with each contingent on previous decisions made. In the case of a 'cold case investigation', for example, an investigator is basing their entire decision-making on the past decisions of previous investigators; that is, decisions not made by them as with 'live/current' investigations (Roach, 2018).

Police decisions are often required in difficult and complex circumstances, often made in a split-second, and based upon incomplete or contradictory information (Roycroft and Roach, 2019). In addition, police officers and police staff are sometimes required to make decisions in circumstances where those involved might be deliberately trying to mislead them, as in the case of interviews with many suspects of crime. It is therefore unsurprising that sometimes decisions made by police do not achieve the best outcomes; for example, deciding that a guilty individual looks innocent or that an innocent individual looks guilty.

For UK police a framework (albeit a very general) is available within which decisions can be questioned or 'examined and challenged', both at the point in time that a decision is being made and afterwards, such as in a review of the decisions by a senior investigating officer (SIO) recorded in their 'decision log', with the benefit of hindsight. This decision-making framework is known as the National Decision Model (NDM) and my version of it is illustrated by Figure 3.1.[12]

The NDM was developed to incorporate six key elements, each highlighting an area for police to consider when making an 'operational decision'. The NDM is suitably generic to be used in any aspect or area of police decision-making (including investigative) but it does not prescribe exactly what and how police decisions should be made, which considering

Figure 3.1: My version of the National Decision Model

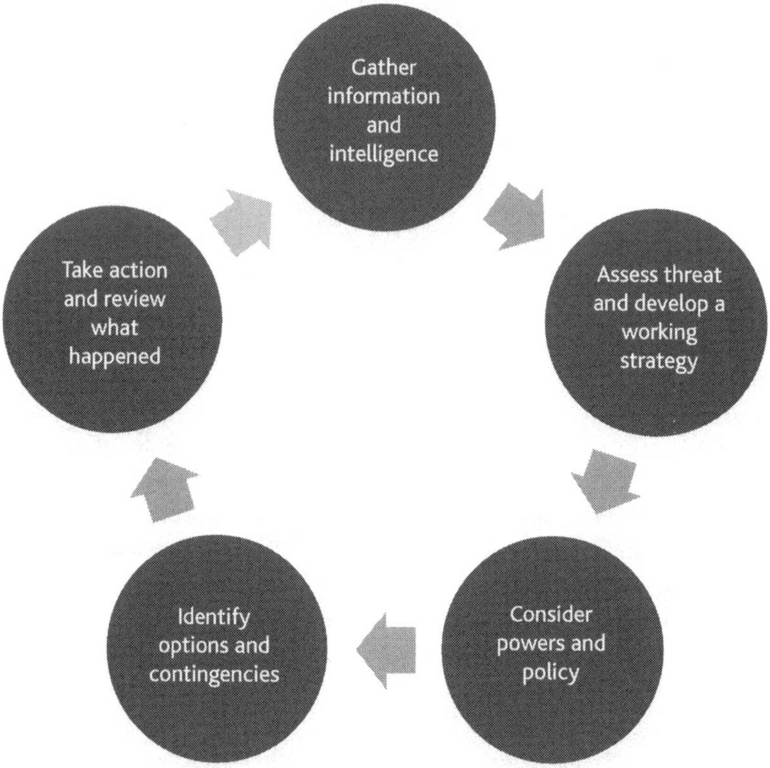

the ever-changing situations and contexts, in which police find themselves in everyday, would be impossible anyway (Roach and Cartwright, 2021).

The Code of Ethics at the heart of the NDM includes the principles of 'fairness' and 'respect', as these are considered important to serving the people appropriately and for maintaining public confidence in the police. It comprises:

- **Accountability** – Answerable for your decisions, actions and omissions
- **Fairness** – Treat people fairly
- **Honesty** – Be truthful and trustworthy
- **Integrity** – Always do the right thing
- **Leadership** – Lead by good example
- **Objectivity** – Make choices on evidence and your best professional judgement
- **Openness** – Be open and transparent in your actions and decisions
- **Respect** – Treat everyone with respect
- **Selflessness** – Act in the public interest

The NDM is therefore more of a decision-making framework within which UK police can situate their decision-making; for example, it encourages them to reflect on the decisions they make and their related actions. Having been mandatory for some years, SIOs have to keep 'decision logs' during their criminal investigations. The primary purpose being one of transparency and accountability for the decisions they make and to help inform 'reviewing officers' about what was done and why. The need for transparency in police decision-making and the subsequent resulting actions was identified as far back as the early 1980s in the report by Sir Lawrence Byford into the Police Handling of the Yorkshire Ripper Case (Byford, 1981).[13] Byford concluded that this had been sadly lacking in the investigation into the murders of 13 women from 1975 to 1981 (for example, see Roach and Pease, 2009).

The NDM does not, of course, replace the need for police to often exercise discretion; for example, in terms of the proportionality of the response, such as whether to help an intoxicated member of the public lying in the street to get home, or to charge them with a Public Order offence. Unfortunately, whether that discretion is a correct judgement is only available with hindsight, but nevertheless, police are called to exercise their judgement/discretion sometimes on an hourly basis (or even sooner) and, to some extent at least, the NDM does serve to help them consider all the options available to them (for example, in law) before doing so.

So, if the NDM is a framework for UK police to make decisions within, is there anything to help them to actually make operational decisions? By way of example, we now briefly look at police decision-making in criminal investigations.

The investigative mindset (or how to think like a detective)

UK officers are routinely provided with several guides and procedural manuals designed to help with decision-making in criminal investigations, the most notable being the *Murder Investigation Manual* (MIM) (Association of Chief Police Officers, 2006. The MIM was developed to help guide SIOs through the numerous processes and procedures necessary to meet, for example, evidential standards, in homicide investigations. The *Core Investigative Doctrine* (ACPO/Centrex 2005) is more generic as it provides guidance to those conducting any type of criminal investigation, but like the MIM it encourages police investigators to adopt an '*investigative mindset*', comprising:

- **A**ccept nothing
- **B**elieve nothing
- **C**hallenge everything

Alas, little more information is given in these two guidance manuals on how to achieve and maintain this investigative mindset, above and beyond 'keeping an open-mind', which is often much easier said than done. There is little doubt, however, that the sentiment behind the ABC advice and investigative mindset is aimed squarely at police recognising and avoiding traps of biased thinking that can have a negative influence on their decision-making and even completely derail criminal investigations.

Enter the importance of psychological research on cognitive bias and how can it negatively influence in investigative decision-making?

Bear traps and pitfalls: cognitive bias and investigative decision-making

The success of a criminal investigation (that is, where a suspect is successfully identified and charged) largely depends on the correct decision-making of the investigator (Fahsing and Ask, 2013; Fahsing, 2018). We do not, however, live in a world which is neither conducive to, nor supportive of, perfect decision-making. Neither do criminal investigators, whose optimal decision-making is often influenced by the many pressures of the job, such as the requirement of expediency over taking one's time, and a competition for limited resources. Given this backdrop, it is rather unsurprising that investigator objectivity has been consistently debilitated (for example, Ask and Granhag, 2007; Fahsing and Ask, 2013) and which has led to numerous examples of miscarriages of justice (see Rossmo (2009) for a good discussion of 'investigative failure' and error with real-case examples).

Gollwitzer (1990) suggests much human decision-making (and consequently often behaviour) to be 'goal directed'. That is, we tend to make decisions with specific goals in mind and there is little doubt that investigative decision-making is any different, with the aim of solving the case and bringing the 'bad guys' to justice. Building on Gollwitzer and colleagues' early work (Gollwitzer, Heckhausen, and Steller, 1990), Fahsing and Ask (2013) tested the cognitive performance of criminal investigators' decision-making across different stages of goal-directed behaviour, and found that when investigators were in a *deliberative mindset*, they were more open-minded and generated a greater number of hypotheses (for example, about what might have happened and why in a crime), than when they adopted a more closed and narrow *implemental mindset*. They conclude that this is important:

> Translated to the investigative setting, it would appear that detectives are better equipped to perform an impartial search for and analysis of investigative information before (that is, in a deliberative mindset), as

opposed to after (that is, in an implemental mindset), a decision has been made to start building a case against the suspect in an investigation. (Fahsing and Ask, 2013, p 156)

Most of the research relating to police investigative decision-making to date focuses on 'criminal investigative failures', where the making of wrong decisions has led to either tragic miscarriages of justice or the culprit not being identified (Rossmo, 2009), such as when an innocent person is wrongly convicted of a crime or where the offender is not identified at all. In both cases there is little hope of the victims or their loved ones achieving justice for the crime committed against them. Consequently, much of the research in this area to date has focused on 'bad' and 'erroneous' investigator decision-making and what causes and influences it. Cognitive bias is often singled out as the main villain of the piece, in a literature replete with examples of how it can and does negatively influence investigative decision-making (for example, see Wright, 2013). Returning to the notorious criminal investigation into the Yorkshire Ripper murders in the North of England between 1975 and 1981, provides numerous examples of how different types of cognitive bias, such as attribution bias, tunnel-vision, and other influential 'heuristics' can negatively impact the outcome of a large criminal investigation (see, for example, Byford, 1981[14]; Rossmo, 2007, 2009; Roach and Pease, 2009). Attribution error is briefly explained in Box 3.3.

Box 3.3: Attribution errors

One of the most pervasive influences of the representativeness heuristic concerns the attribution of victim blaming. Lee Ross defined the *Fundamental Attribution Error* (FAE) as the tendency for people to overemphasise personal characteristics and ignore situational factors in judging others' behaviour, often resulting in cognitive bias and error (Ross, 1977). If, for example, I am constantly late to a lecture then I may reason away (or excuse) my tardiness on the bus being late or on my alarm clock failing to work properly. In other words, I am favouring a situational (external) explanation for my poor timekeeping, over any internal explanations such as being a poor timekeeper. FAE can represent bias in two directions, however – although I might excuse my lateness based on situational factors seemingly beyond my control, the class of students that have been consistency punctual to my lectures may see it a different way. Either way, the outcome is the same (that is, I was late), but the reason (or blame) depends on the viewpoint taken; that is, whether you are the 'actor' (me) or the 'observer' (the students). Unsurprisingly, this is known as the 'actor–observer' effect and displays bias from two viewpoints.

Put simply, common sense suggests that we can improve the efficacy and effectiveness of investigative decision-making by reducing the effects and influence of cognitive bias, but of course equally it can also be improved by identifying good decision-making (Roach and Cartwright, 2021). That said, we finish the chapter with an illustration of how cognitive bias can have a negative effect on police decision-making commonly referred to as 'victim blaming', with the aim of showing how psychology can inform future good police decision-making.

Victim blaming in sexual offence cases

Victim blaming is a perception that the victim of a crime is in some way responsible for their victimisation. A first, and often cited, common characteristic implicated in accusations of police victim blaming has been the degree to which the victim is considered to have been under the influence of alcohol at the time of the sexual offence. In a US-based study, Schuller and Stewart (2000) found that the more a victim of a sexual offence (namely, rape) was perceived to have been intoxicated, the more they were blamed and the less the alleged perpetrator was. In an Australian study, however, based on Shuller and Stewart's (2000) study, Goodman-Delahunty and Graham (2011) found no relationship between perceived levels of victim intoxication and victim blaming. The authors suggest that this difference is probably explained by the procedural differences in the research methods used, or because of the different culturally driven attitudes between US and Australian participants towards women drinking alcohol (Sleath and Bull, 2017).

Another characteristic identified as influencing police victim blaming in sexual offence cases is the existence of a prior relationship between the victim and perpetrator (Areh, Mesko, & Umek, 2009). For example, research suggests that victims of acquaintance rape appear to be attributed more blame by police than victims of stranger rape (Sleath & Bull, 2012) with victims of 'marital rape' most likely to be blamed by police for their victimisation (Areh et al, 2009).

A third characteristic concerns the gender of the victim, where Davies et al (2009), for example, found in their UK study that male victims were more likely to be attributed blame by police than female victims.

The perceived credibility of a witness has been identified as an important factor in the attribution of victim blaming by police in sexual offence cases. Page (2008a, 2008b, 2010) found that police judgements of victim credibility depended upon what type of person the victim was described as. For example, when described as a 'sex worker', 44 per cent of police participants reported that they would be unlikely to believe the victim had been raped.

How witnesses behave emotionally has also been identified as a common rape myth. For example, Bollingmo, Wessel, Eilertsen, and Magnussen (2008), in a study with Norwegian police, found that victim credibility was affected by the emotions that a female victim displayed when giving her statement. Those displaying negative emotions were taken as indicative of an upset, presumably 'real victim', with more neutral (for example, shallow affect) or positive emotions (for example, not appearing upset) being indicative of a relaxed victim and presumably less believable. Similar findings have been reported by Ask and Landstrom (2010) with a sample of Swedish police trainees, seemingly re-enforcing the existence of the 'rape myth' of 'emotional and behavioural congruence' outlined previously.

Finally, additional accusations of police victim blaming identified by the research relate to the presence or absence of evidence. Venema (2014) found that police perceptions of victim credibility were linked to the level of detail that they provided in their witness statement and the presence of forensic evidence (for example, physical injury).

In terms of psychology helping to improve police decision-making, as the gatekeepers of the criminal justice system, cognitive bias such as victim blaming can have a detrimental effect on police decision-making, which does not simply impact on the making of operational and investigative decisions, but more importantly on the administration and functioning of justice itself. Again, psychological research and policing need to work closer together to improve police decision-making and reduce bias in this important area of criminal investigation.

Chapter summary

This chapter began with a brief exploration of how human beings make decisions, with reference to evolutionary psychology and the pioneering research on cognitive bias conducted by psychologists including Kahneman and Tversky. Next, how police make decisions was explored, including an introduction to Problem-Orientated Policing (POP), the SARA problem-solving model, and discussion of the National Decision Model, developed to help UK police make decisions, before concluding with a focus on how cognitive bias can have a negative influence on criminal investigations, with reference to the research on accusations of police victim blaming in the investigation of sexual offences.

Further reading

Association of Chief Police Officers of England and Wales (ACPO) (2006) *Murder Investigation Manual*, Bramshill: National Centre for Policing Excellence.

Fahsing, I. and Ask, K. (2013) 'Decision-making and decisional tipping points in homicide investigations: an interview study of British and Norwegian detectives', *Journal of Investigative Psychology and Offender Profiling*, 10(2): 155–65.

Rossmo, D.K. (ed) (2009) *Criminal Investigative Failures*, Baton Rouge: CRC Press.

Stelfox, P. (2008) *Criminal Investigation*, Cullompton: Willan.

Suggested resources

Problem-Solving Approach – Pop Centre website: https://popcenter.asu.edu/content/what-pop

Criminal Investigative Guidance: https://www.college.police.uk/app/investigation

National decision Model: https://www.app.college.police.uk/app-content/national-decision-model/the-national-decision-model/

4

Challenging common police perceptions of career criminals and serious offenders

Introduction

This chapter is short deliberately. Its purpose is to challenge police thinking on criminal careers and career criminals (Roach and Pease, 2013). It exists to provide the theoretical and supporting research to influence police thinking towards the offence versatility of serious criminals. Its purpose is to unashamedly pave the way for the next which introduces the Self-Selection Policing (SSP) approach. For the reader to accept the psychology and research evidence behind the SSP approach, they must first be convinced that serious offenders tend to be more versatile than specialist with the crimes they commit. If you cannot be swayed towards this way of thinking (I once had a student who could not accept that serious criminals also commit less serious crimes) then it is probably advisable for you to skip Chapter 5 and move straight to Chapter 6.

In short, this chapter attempts to use psychological understanding and academic research to challenge current police perceptions of serious criminals as 'crime specialists'; that is, the prevailing psychology of police officers that a serious criminal will only commit the same type of crime.

Understanding the crime and offending patterns of serious offenders is of obvious importance to both police psychology (that is, decision-making) and to police practice, particularly in the area of criminal investigation. The case will be made here, that for although current police thinking leans heavily towards a perception of serious criminals as 'crime specialists' (that is, they only stick to one type of crime and that is serious) most of the research evidence points in the opposite direction, towards serious criminals being 'crime versatile' (that is, they tend to commit a wider range of crimes including 'minor' ones).

The reader is forgiven for not accepting immediately why such a seemingly small change in police thinking, from viewing serious criminals as crime specialists to serious criminals as crime 'versatilists' (if this is indeed a word) as a big deal for police psychology, but a case will be made for why police need to switch their thinking by demonstrating how such a shift can open up additional investigative avenues with which to identify active, serious criminality.

As stated, the principal aim of this chapter is to pave the way 'psychologically' for the next, which introduces the SSP approach. SSP is an additional means by which active, serious offenders can be identified by the minor offences they commit. If a shift to viewing serious offenders as 'crime versatile' is not achieved, then adopting such an approach becomes instantly irrelevant. Indeed, as we shall see in Chapter 5, several current police 'psychological and policy barriers' need to be overcome, before the SSP approach can be accepted into UK policing. With this chapter we concentrate on what has been identified as a sizeable obstacle in police psychology – challenging current police thinking on the offending patterns of serious criminals (Roach and Pease, 2013). My apologies if I have somewhat laboured the point.

We begin with a brief examination of current police thinking pertaining to serious criminals and current methods by which they are identified, before presenting a case for why this needs to change.

Identifying serious criminals by existing and traditional police methods

Traditionally, police have tended to identify serious offenders either from information supplied by the public, and/or by the targeting of known offenders. Information supplied by the public, particularly in the form of witness statements, is undoubtedly the most frequent means by which cases are progressed (Roach and Pease, 2016). In the second, commonly referred to as 'the usual suspects' method of criminal investigation, a case is constructed against a 'known offender(s)', especially those known to have 'built up a set of previous convictions and have been well known to the local police' (Maguire, 2008, p 435). In the case of a sexual offence, for example, it is understandably common practice for police to consult the 'sex offenders register'[1] in an initial attempt to generate potential suspect leads. Although personally I have no criticism of these approaches, the question begged is 'are there other ways by which serious offenders might be identified?' Even the less astute and more cynical of readers will have gathered that I think the answer to be 'yes'!

The strengths and weaknesses of the usual suspect approach are not debated here, although it does rather assume that those targeted are indeed (1) criminally active and (2) necessitates the possession of accurate knowledge of offenders and their offending patterns, which research by Townsley and Pease (2008) has shown police perceptions of prolific offenders on their patch, to be at best debatable. For example, if the findings that police thinking on who the most prolific burglars are in their area is indeed inaccurate, and this holds for other types of serious crime, then subsequent investigations do rather run the risk of degenerating into a complete waste of police time as they will often be chasing the wrong people, or even worse it can lead to justified claims of harassment by the mis-targeted. A nod to this argument will suffice here, as although the usual suspects approach can (and does) lead on many occasions to a successful conclusion, it is far from an exact science and is worryingly considered by many to be a blatant breech of human rights. Arguably, it is sometimes used as evidence of 'lazy' police thinking (Roach and Pease, 2016).

The case for the defence: research and theoretical support shifting to the idea of the crime-versatile serious offender

To quote the British actress Dame Julie Andrews, 'let's start at the very beginning' with Blumstein, Cohen, Roth, and Visher's classic work *Criminal Careers and Career Criminals* (1986a, 1986b) which provided one of the first major empirical demonstrations of how limited the degree of specialisation in most criminal careers, and so by implication, is the high degree of versatility generally found. Other researchers since have consistently confirmed this central finding of offence versatility (for example, Farrington, 1986; Blumstein, Cohen, Das, and Moitra, 1988; Gottfredson and Hirschi, 1990) irrespective of whether self-report, arrest, conviction, or reconviction data is used (for example, Soothill, Fitzpatrick, and Francis, 2009; Harris, Smallbone, Dennison, and Knight, 2009). Versatile-offender thinking has, for example, more recently been found consistent with research on what might commonly be perceived to be the most specialised end of serious criminality, the criminal histories of 'stranger sexual killers' (Greenall and Wright, 2015).

David Farrington and colleagues eloquently summarised the findings of the criminal careers research back in 1988: 'There is a small but significant degree of specialisation, superimposed on a great deal of versatility' (Farrington, Snyder, and Finnegan 1988, p 483). The evidence post-1988 continues to support the perception that prolific and serious criminals are likely to be versatile in their offending, committing an array of different types of crime as and when opportunities to do so arise (for example, Cunliffe and Shepherd, 2007; Roach and Pease, 2013).

Box 4.1 presents further evidence that sex offenders, considered by most to be the epitome of the 'specialised offender' (probably as their motivation is sexual rather than financial) are also crime versatile in terms of the variety of criminality for which they are convicted.

Less surprising perhaps than the acceptance that sex offenders tend to be more crime versatile than specialised in their offending, is that those who persistently (or prolifically) commit crime have consistently been found to be

Box 4.1: Are sex offenders crime versatile?

Those who commit sexually motivated offences are considered by many to represent the most specialised of criminals. Why? Well, for example, these individuals are encouraged to engage with treatments and programmes developed to deal specifically with their sexual offending, generally segregated within prisons away from other 'types' of prisoners, and are placed on a 'register' if and when they are released back into society. Can you think of any other types of crime in which those who perpetrate them are treated so differently?

Soothill, Francis, Sanderson, and Ackerley (2000) found in a study of over 7,000 UK sex offenders evidence of differences in offence specialisation and versatility between different groups of sexual offender; for example, males convicted of underage sexual intercourse (statutory rape) displayed an offending versatility which took in the full spectrum of criminality, whereas those convicted of indecency between males, although infrequent, tended to be reconvicted for the same offence.

versatile in their offending (for example, Cohen and Felson, 2008; Kempf, 1987; Blumstein et al, 1988 Farrington, 1988; LeBlanc and Frechette, 1989; Gottfredson and Hirschi,1990; Tarling, 1993; Mazerolle et al, 2000). Piquero (2000) found frequent violent offenders indistinguishable from non-violent offenders in respect of their future criminal careers, especially in terms of their versatility of criminality/offending.

Theoretical support for the versatile offender

For those readers interested in whether criminological theories favour notions of the versatile offender, then support is provided by *Environmental Criminology*, an approach whereby it is the environment and context which are the critical determinants of whether a crime is committed or not (and which and what crimes are committed) and not simply focusing on why people commit crime. It is suggested by environmental criminologists that it is 'Opportunity that makes the thief' (Felson and Clarke, 1998) with a motivated offender as a given. Without an opportunity to do so, even the most motivated criminal on a desert island will struggle to do so. Personally, I am more convinced that 'Opportunity makes a theft more likely' is probably nearer the mark, because, and as shall be discussed in Chapter 7, an opportunity is only an opportunity if you perceive it to be so. See Box 4.2 for a worked demonstration of whether you consider proflic and serious offenders to be versatile in their offending.

Box 4.2: Why seeing prolific and persistent offenders as crime versatile makes sense

What do you think that an individual whose last crime was burglary, who comes across a car with its key fob still left in the ignition and a laptop on the back seat, is most likely to do?

1. Take the car?
2. Take the laptop?
3. Take both the car and the laptop?
4. Consider themselves a burglar and not a car thief, and so carry on their merry way and not act on this crime opportunity?

I'm guessing you answered yes to 1–3 but not to 4.

Environmental criminology rests on two main theoretical underpinnings, *Rational Choice Theory* (Cornish and Clarke, 1986, 2008) and *Routine Activity Theory* (Cohen and Felson, 1979; Felson, 1994, 1998; Cohen and Felson, 2008). Rational Choice Theory identifies how offenders calculate decisions to commit crime, and Routine Activity Theory explains how offenders come across criminal opportunities. Both are explained further in Box 4.3.

Box 4.3: Rational Choice Theory and Routine Activity Theory

Rational Choice Theory (RCT) states that individuals will offend if they consider the environment and situation conducive to do so. Individuals are likely to be versatile in their offending as opportunity plays a role and as opportunities vary, versatility is anticipated. Also active, serious offenders are highly unlikely to stop at committing minor offences as, by definition, minor crime generally carries little risk of serious punishment.

Routine Activity Theory (RAT) also identifies environments and situations as important in the crime commission of a crime, with offenders acting on opportunities to commit crime as they go about their daily 'routine' activities, such as going to the gym or the pub. As such, offenders are versatile in their offences, acting (or not) on opportunities as they present themselves rather than as dedicated crime specialists. Cohen and Felson (1979) although initially concerned with crimes of a predatory nature, go on to make little distinction between a routine activities explanation of serious and minor offending, their theory being one for all crime.

Hopefully by this point the reader is at least beginning to be convinced (or else bored into submission) that the evidence points to serious offenders being more likely to be crime versatilists than specialists in only one type of crime. That is not to say that they may not prefer engaging in certain types of crime; for example, they might favour committing burglary, but also regularly engage in committing theft from or of cars, or 'shop-lifting' (that is, stealing from shops). Put simply, they will be more driven to act on crime opportunities as they occur for them, rather than only acting on those they plan.

So why is this important whether police see serious criminals as crime specialists or versatile offenders? This is the question to which we now turn.

Police perceptions of serious criminals: the need for a 'nudge'

So, do police tend to view serious offenders as offence versatile or as specialists? One important manifestation of what is known as the representativeness heuristic is confirmation bias, whereby initial partially or non-relevant information (in this case the prior officially processed offence) restricts an investigator's search space inappropriately (Roach and Pease, 2013). For example, those with convictions for burglary will not be considered as suspects for a robbery because this reflects a different type of criminality. As highlighted in the previous chapter, confirmation bias has been implicated in many cases of criminal investigative failure (see Rossmo, 2009).

Research evidence suggests that police tend (as do most probably the public) to overestimate offence homogeneity; that is, they tend to view serious offenders to be crime specialists. In a study of police estimates of next offences in criminal careers, Roach and Pease (2013) found overwhelmingly that police participants considered an individual's previous offence type as the best predictor of their likely future offence type, irrespective of the type of offence history that was presented. Put simply, they found that whatever the first offence type, participants predicted that most likely next offence would be of the same type (for example, for offender with previous offence of robbery the most likely next offence predicted was again robbery). Indeed, for an overwhelming majority of pairings of past and possible future offence types, the average for participant predictions of offence homogeneity was more than 50 per cent. When compared with real data gleaned from reconviction studies, a more modest 30 per cent was found (for example, see Cunliffe and Shepherd, 2007). Although Roach and Pease (2013) do acknowledge some difficulties with directly comparing participant predictions of offence homogeneity with 'official' reconviction data, as far as reconvictions go, and in line with the criminal careers literature generally, offence homogeneity appears actually to be low (Farrington, 1988; Cunliffe and Shepherd, 2007; Roach and Pease, 2013). This perception is appeared to be incongruent (or even at odds) with over-estimated levels often held by police in the Roach and Pease (2013) study.

Why is this probable misperception of the offending patterns of serious criminals by police so important? It represents a likely psychological barrier which continues to influence both police practice and the thinking of senior police and policymakers, serving to hobble the adoption of additional approaches to identifying active, serious offenders, who are based on the perception of such offenders as offence versatile. SSP is one such approach and is the focus of the next chapter (Roach, 2007a; Roach and Pease, 2016).

Chapter summary

This chapter has challenged the prevailing police psychology of the crime specialist offender, particularly the perceived narrow offending patterns of serious criminals. Both research on criminal careers and theories including Rational Choice Theory and Routine Activities Theory, support the stance that police thinking should shift from seeing serious offenders as offence specialist to being 'offence versatile' (Roach and Pease, 2013). Indeed, dedicated research suggests that a shift in police psychology around criminal careers is needed so that serious criminals might be better targeted and identified by all the crimes that they commit, big or small, in terms of seriousness. A premise very much at the heart of the next chapter on the SSP approach to identifying active, serious offenders, from the minor crimes that they commit.

Further reading

Blumstein, A., Cohen, J., Das, S., and Moitra, S.D. (1988) 'Specialisation and seriousness during adult criminal careers', *Journal of Quantitative Criminology*, 4(4): 303–45.

Clarke, R.V.G. (ed) (1997) *Situational Crime Prevention: Successful Studies* (2nd edn), Albany, NY: Harrow and Heston.

Cohen, L. and Felson, M. (2008) 'The routine activity approach', in R. Wortley and L. Mazerolle (eds) *Environmental Criminology and Crime Analysis*, Cullompton: Willan, pp 70–7.

Cunliffe, J. and Shepherd, A. (2007) *Re-offending of adults: results from the 2004 cohort. Home Office Statistical Bulletin 06/04*, London: Home office.

Roach, J. and Pease, K. (2013) 'Police overestimation of criminal career homogeneity', *Journal of Investigative Psychology and Offender Profiling*, 11(2): 164–78.

Suggested resources

For information on environmental criminology, see https://popcenter.asu.edu/

5

Self-Selection Policing

Introduction

In this chapter the SSP approach (Roach, 2007a, 2007b, 2017, 2018; Roach and Pease, 2016) will be introduced, whereby it is posited that current police means of identifying active, serious criminals can be enhanced by also focusing on the minor crimes that they commit. The argument made is that a growing body of research shows that if police are encouraged to adopt the SSP approach into their 'policing armoury', then more active, serious criminals will be uncovered and brought to justice. A big claim admittedly!

The chapter concludes with some suggestions for how police can best employ and implement SSP and a checklist is provided to help those interested in conducting SSP interventions of their own.

Traditional ways of uncovering bad guys

Approaches to policing do not come much simpler than SSP. Its purpose is the identification of active, serious offenders by targeting the more minor criminal offences that they also commit, however minor these may be. It can be argued that the self-selection approach rests on firmer ground 'legally' than the targeting of 'usual suspects' for example because of the similar way they commit the same type of crime (that is, modus operandi) or based simply on the same type of previous conviction(s) (Roach and Pease, 2016). The SSP approach seeks to identify those minor, often routine, offences which stand as reliable indicators of more serious current criminality (Roach, 2007a, 2007b; Roach and Pease, 2016; Roach, 2018). SSP is concerned therefore with the identification of those minor offences that are disproportionately committed by active, serious offenders (that is, most frequently compared with other minor offences).

Chiming deliberately with the previous chapter, SSP is based upon the simple premise that 'those who do big bad things also do little bad things' (Roach, 2007a). The logic being that if police scrutiny of certain, specific, minor offences is increased then this is likely to assist in the identification of active, serious criminals. By certain minor offences, I mean those committed most frequently by active, serious offenders, as it goes without saying that a vast majority of minor (or lesser) offences will be committed by the likes of you and I and not by 'heavy-duty offenders'.[1]

Nor am I suggesting that police should bring down the full weight of the law upon those who commit minor offences, such as parking a vehicle illegally on double-yellow lines, in a 'zero-tolerance' type approach to crime reduction; on the contrary, how police proceed with such infractions of the law are a matter of professional discretion – for example, deciding on a simple verbal warning and NFA (No Further Action). That is not for me to say. But what I am making the case for is while those who commit minor offences are in the spotlight, then police are politely encouraged to take this opportunity to scrutinise them and to dig a little deeper into their lives, with a simple 'thank you and have a good day' if nothing untoward is found. The reason being that they may have inadvertently uncovered an active, serious criminal and not simply a normally law-abiding member of the public. At the very least it would be rude to not oblige serious offenders when they commit minor offences; for example, when multiple murderer Joel Rifkin was stopped for not having State plates on his vehicle, police found a body in the back of his pick-up truck (Roach and Pease, 2016). Perhaps most importantly, identifying specific minor 'trigger offences' indicative of likely concurrent serious criminality, will encourage police to think that the person they have stopped for that minor offence might be a serious criminal, and indeed be forewarned and prepared for someone who would not think twice about using violence against them. Police officers in the US, for example, are all too often injured or killed by those they stop for minor traffic violations (Roach and Pease, 2016).

The identification of active, serious criminals therefore constitutes this chapter's focus, and we now move to take a brief look at the psychology behind SSP and why it should serve as a useful additional detection tool in the police armoury.

Psychology and Self-Selection Policing

For SSP to be a credible proposition, Roach and Pease (2016) suggest that three pivotal premises that must first be supported.

1. Active serious offenders are 'crime versatile' (as proposed in the previous chapter).
2. Active, serious offenders do not stop at committing more minor offences.
3. Identifiable links exist between active serious offenders and certain more minor offences.

Hopefully the reader was at least partially convinced by the evidence presented in the previous chapter, that serious criminals tend to be more versatile with the offences they commit than specialised (point 1). Let us look at further evidence of this from two different perspectives: first from the more sensational and arguably 'un-scientific' perpective, and then back to Earth with the less sensational (but more reliable) 'empirical research and theoretical support'.

Self-Selection Policing works: some sensational evidence

Arguably, the most extreme examples of the versatility of serious offenders are cases where notorious repeat (serial) killers and rapists have been identified in the first instance, not as a direct result of long and protracted high-profile police investigations, but because they were caught committing offences of a much more routine and less serious nature. A few of my favourite examples are presented in Box 5.1 for the more intrigued reader.

Such examples of 'self-selection' must not simply be dismissed as mere instances of a criminal's 'bad luck'. Why? Because to be detected of a minor

---

Box 5.1: Famous cases of offence versatility

- The notorious 18th-century highwayman (armed robber) Richard 'Dick Turpin' was wanted for a string of crimes, including murder. Turpin was apprehended and imprisoned for the lesser offence of stealing a horse, but the authorities were not aware of the significance of this arrest for several weeks, until he wrote a letter to his brother saying that he was glad that they did not know that he was actually Dick Turpin! When they finally realised who he was he was hanged as a murderer.
- UK serial murderer Peter Sutcliffe (AKA the Yorkshire Ripper) who brutally killed at least 13 women, was identified because he was found to have false number (registration) plates on his car. Presumably, he committed this minor offence to maintain anonymity from the manhunt launched to identify him.
- US convicted killer Charles Manson was arrested after police were called to his house on suspicion of him having committed offences of criminal damage.
- The serial killer 'Son of Sam' David Berkowitz was arrested after a parking ticket put him at the scene of one of his horrendous crimes.
- In 2013, five men from the West Midlands were convicted of preparing an act of terrorism. They had planned to set off a bomb at a rally organised by the English Defence League, in Dewsbury, West Yorkshire. The men had travelled in two cars with the intent of killing, but had arrived late, after the rally had finished. On their way back home, one of the cars was stopped for not having valid insurance (identified by a police Automatic Number Plate Recognition System on the M11). As a consequence, their car was impounded and, when later searched, police found a bomb and several guns in the boot.

Source: Roach and Pease, 2016

crime, one must commit it in the first place. Luck has nothing to do with their uncovering and only really it is good luck for serious criminals if SSP is not adopted, as they have been lucky enough to get away with another crime, however small. It suffices to say here that SSP demands a change to the psychological framing of such notorious events from one of a criminal's bad luck or 'an unfortunate accident' (for example, a police officer made a lucky stop) to tangible opportunities to identify and apprehend active, serious offenders.

All well and good I hear the yet-to-be-convinced reader say, but serial murderers are rare and disproportionately focused upon by the media and a fascinated public. Is there more credible scientific evidence that serious criminals commit minor crimes? You bet there is.

The next challenge to establishing the credibility of SSP as a viable approach for identifying active, serious criminals by the minor offences they commit, is to identify which minor offences serve best as reliable indicators of, 'or trigger offences' for, serious, concurrent criminality. After all, there are hundreds (if not thousands) of possible minor offences (in UK criminal law alone) to choose from.

We begin with offences which may not have been badged as SSP 'trigger offences' at the time that the research was conducted (well we hadn't invented the term yet) but which in retrospect are clearly within the reach of SSP, with 'those who do big bad things also doing little bad things' (Roach 2007; Roach and Pease, 2016; Roach, 2018). Some of this research is presented in Box 5.2.

Box 5.2: Two early examples of Self-Selection Policing-like thinking

1. Kelling and Coles discovered that a substantial minority of 'Squeegee merchants' (people who clean the windshield/windscreen of your motor vehicle without you asking them, when you stop in traffic, and demand payment) in New York, also had outstanding warrants for felony offences. Thus, when an officer served a ticket for 'squeegeeing', then that officer could make an immediate arrest (Kelling and Coles, 1995, p 143).
2. The New York Transit Police found that by preventing individuals who jumped ticket turnstiles to avoid paying, a general drop in crime in the subway and trains occurred. The fall in crime was attributed to fare evaders also being those that committed many of the other offences (Maple, 1999). Turnstile jumpers therefore were self-selecting themselves as likely candidates for police attention for more serious types of criminality.

Source: Roach and Pease, 2016

In a study of burglary, Jacqui Schneider found an unanticipated but identifiable link between shoplifting and burglary. From her research she concluded that shop theft played an instrumental role in the offending patterns of prolific burglars (Schneider, 2005). Interviews conducted with 50 prolific burglars revealed that 44 (88 per cent) admitted to committing shop theft. Of these 26 did so daily and a further 8 did so 'several times a week'. Only 6 burglars claimed they had never stolen from shops, leading Schneider to conclude, 'That shop thieves be policed as though they were burglars on their day off rather than shop thieves pure and simple' (2005, p 3). Such examples of minor offences linking to more serious offending therefore lends evidential support to SSP's three pivotal premises

1. acceptance of the idea of the versatile offender;
2. acceptance of the idea that serious offenders will also commit minor offences; and
3. acceptance that certain minor offences, such as shoplifting, can be indicative of active serious concurrent criminality.

Self-Selection Policing works: supporting empirical research evidence (the less sensational)

Serious criminals and driving offences

As a Chief Constable of West Midlands Police (UK) once said, 'Not all drivers are criminals, but most criminals are drivers' (Roach and Pease, 2016).

Willett's 1964 book *Criminal on the Road* was one of the first to suggest a link between those committing traffic offences and other types of crime. Not until Gerry Rose's seminal study of the minor-major offending link in the year 2000 (no doubt inspired by the accessible parking bay study by Chenery et al, 1999) was research published explicitly dedicated to analysis of the broader criminal histories of serious road traffic offenders (Rose, 2000). Rose tested the common perception that those committing such offences were no more criminal than the average motorist (for example, see Steer and Carr-Hill, 1967). Rose's UK-based study entailed an investigation of the nature of serious traffic offending and the extent to which it is 'interwoven with mainstream criminal offending' (Rose, 2000, p 67).

In the Rose (2000) study, a large sample of UK serious traffic offenders were divided into three groups: drink drivers, disqualified drivers, and dangerous drivers, based on current known convictions and previous incidents. As a group, serious traffic offenders were found to be predominantly white males, with the age profiles of *dangerous drivers* and *disqualified drivers* found to be like those of more mainstream offenders, with some 60–75 per cent aged between 18 and 32 years (although those in the drink driver category were found to be older) with those from lower social groups found to be more likely to have committed vehicle licence and car insurance offences. Risk factors such as family, schooling, and peer groups were found to correlate significantly with serious traffic offences, so again mirroring those common involved with other types of criminality (Rose, 2000).

Interestingly, Rose (2000) also found strong elements of consistency with the findings of other studies. Steer and Carr-Hill (1967), for example, had identified a distinction between 'dishonest offenders' and 'driving offenders', with the 'dishonest' group including disqualified drivers and those driving without a licence or insurance, closely linked to mainstream criminality in the findings of a simultaneous interview study (Rose 2000). Rose (2000) also found supporting evidence for Steer and Carr-Hill's (1967) 'driving offenders' as not simply constituting 'unlucky' members of the public, but more likely to be serious offenders. For example, drink drivers were estimated to be twice as likely to have criminal records than members of the wider public. Dangerous and reckless drivers were found to be even more likely to be involved in concurrent criminality, especially car theft.

Rose's (2000) findings were also consistent with Suggs' (1998) smaller study of motor offenders (including theft of vehicles and driving while disqualified) who attended several motor projects run by the National Probation Service for England and Wales (now the National Prison and Probation Service). Suggs' results indicated that these motoring/driving offenders were far from being 'crime specialists', as they had convictions for numerous other types of crime, such as: theft (75 per cent), burglary (60 per cent), and violence against the person (30 per cent). The data also showed that reconvictions (over a two-year period) commonly included non-motoring offences, such as: theft (39 per cent), burglary (25 per cent), and violence against the person (15 per cent) – strongly suggesting that this group of driving/motoring offenders was ensconced in versatile criminal careers. Smerdon and South (1997) offer further support as they found, from a small study of people that had driven without motor insurance, that 'Kevin', a principal focus of the case-study research, had been arrested for an incident of robbery soon after they had interviewed him.

A first piece of UK-based dedicated SSP research was a local study of illegal parking in accessible parking bays when other 'legal' spaces were available (Chenery, Henshaw, and Pease, 1999). The findings were that one in five (20 per cent) of those who had committed this offence had outstanding warrants for the arrest of the registered keeper of the vehicle, or other characteristics which would have 'excited immediate police attention', compared with 2 per cent for those in legally parked adjacent cars (Chenery, Henshaw, and Pease 1999). The annoying and antisocial behaviour of illegally parking in accessible parking bays when adjacent bays are available should be considered one of the first 'trigger offences' for uncovering active serious criminality. It never ceases to amaze me how many cops have heard about this study but have never put it into policing practice. We will deal with the some of the potential and obvious barriers to the wider adoption of SSP into UK policing practice a little later in this chapter.

Wellsmith and Guille (2005), in their assessment of the suitability of parking fixed penalty notices (FPN) as a trigger offence indicative of concurrent criminality, concluded those single offences were unreliable indicators of serious offending; however, repeat FPN offences were found to be modestly associated with concurrent criminality, relative to a random group selected from an electoral role (the list of those eligible to vote in elections in a given district or ward).

In the North of England, Townsley and Pease (2003), in collaboration with Merseyside Police, the DVLA, and a local Merseyside taxi association, conducted a first trial of SSP on the roads, by overseeing a vehicle inspection programme. Over the course of a four-hour period, on a selected day, any driver seen not wearing a seatbelt would be pulled over. Where the 'non-use of seatbelt' self-selection trigger was used for private vehicles (n = 62), 3 per cent of drivers were immediately arrested, 14.5 per cent were found to have committed a Vehicle Excise Licence offence (VEL) (that is, they did not have the required licence (that is, had not paid the required annual tax) for the vehicle they were driving to be using UK roads) and 11 per cent where issued a dangerous 'unroadworthy vehicle' prohibition notice. A staggering 50 per cent of taxis (and private-hire cars) stopped during the exercise were issued with vehicle defect and stop notices, where the licensed for private-hire plate was removed until such time as the vehicle was deemed to be now 'roadworthy' (that is, safe). By way of comparison, an operation was also conducted which did not see police use the non-use of seat-belt trigger offence, where instead they stopped all vehicles of a specific age, at a specific time of day (selected for likelihood of theft). Those found offending amounted to approximately 5 per cent, demonstrating that the non-use of seat-belt trigger had a much greater 'hit rate' in terms of identifying offenders, than random stop checks, by at least a factor of ten (Townsley and Pease, 2003).

As I write, a section of the Metropolitan Police is currently conducting a trial whereby they compare the outcome of current routine police practice for identifying active, serious offending (that is, based on hunches and 'gut feelings') with an SSP approach to stopping vehicles for specific minor traffic offences. I'm not a betting man, but I am quietly confident that the result will provide further support to the SSP approach.

In a further driver-/driving-related SSP study, Roach (2007b) explored the possibility of police use of the Home Office Road Transport 1 (HO/RT1) as a potential SSP 'trigger offence' for uncovering active, serious criminals. The HO/RT1 is what used to be issued when police stopped a vehicle and the driver who did not produce (hence, the nickname 'producer') the required legal vehicle and driving documentation. Said driver was then compelled to show the required documentation at a police station of their choice within seven days. The original hypothesis was not that being issued with a HO/RT1 in and of itself would signify serious criminality, but that non-compliance with the rather simple and innocuous legal requirement of producing vehicle and driver documents (for example, driver's licence and insurance certificate) at a police station for verification within seven days, might. Ergo, that those entrenched in criminal careers would not wish to draw attention to themselves and knew full well that to not do so would likely end in little or no repercussion.

Why would you not comply unless you have something to hide? Does non-compliance signify a general underlying contempt for criminal justice and the police? In short, was it that the 'little bad thing' of failing to produce could be a flag for the 'big bad things' which they were also engaging in. Analysis of over 120 HO/RT1 issued in Lancashire on a specific day, the findings showed that those who did not fully, or only partially, comply with the HO/RT1 (referred to here as 'no shows') were found to be significantly more likely than those that complied (referred to here as 'showed') to have a previous criminal record (Roach, 2007b). 'No shows' were found more likely to have offence histories that comprised two or more offences, than the 'showed group'. Indeed, many had three or more crimes recorded. The 'no shows' were also found to have committed more serious (often violent) offences than the 'showed' group. Lastly, and possibly most significantly, the results of a linear (step-wise) regression analysis indicated that the 'no shows' had recorded offences more recently than the 'showed', with many having committed a serious offence(s) within six months of being issued with the HO/RT1, suggesting that they were ensconced in criminal careers as their offending was more current than historical. Bingo!

Alas, the window for using HO/RT1 non-compliance as an SSP 'trigger offence' for uncovering active, serious criminality has now closed, as UK police no longer use HO/RT1s to require vehicle drivers to produce. Instead, access to databases with which to check if drivers have the correct vehicle tax, driving licence, and so on at the point of stopping them is possible. Although this is undoubtedly progress in some ways, no less than the reduction of a need for 'producer' paper and so the saving of trees, and the fact that it increases the number of people detected for 'driving illegally' that can be stopped and dealt with immediately. However, and here is my lament, it had the negative effect of removing the opportunity for serious criminals not to comply and produce (our no-show group) and with it the opportunity for police scrutiny of those that do not 'comply' probably because they are career criminals. Remember, it was the failure to comply (that is, to present the necessary documents at a police station) which proved to be the trigger for uncovering concurrent criminality, not the lack of suitable documents. As such, the opportunity for police to identify HO/RT1 non-compliance as self-selection for more serious criminality has been lost. I'm equally sad (or maybe I'm even sadder or just sad myself?) in that I also opine the loss of the vehicle tax disc for similar reasons, displaying an out-of-date vehicle tax disc being clear for all to see and worthy of scrutinising the registered keeper of the vehicle for concurrent criminality. But that is probably just me, so we shall move on.

In a study of 50 people convicted of driving while disqualified, Roach (2017) found that they had a total of 704 recorded convictions between them, with an average of 14 recorded offences per disqualified driver (range = 0–84 offences, SD = 17.63 offences). Of the 50 disqualified drivers, 43 (86 per cent) had previous criminal convictions for offences other than the index offence of driving while disqualified which had led to their inclusion in the study. The range of offence types found (that is, category versatility) for each of the 43 when discounting the original index offence of driving while disqualified, ranged from 1 to 10 different offence categories from 12 possible (mean = 4.9 and SD = 2.8). Moreover, 60 per cent had convictions for between 4 and 10 offence categories, indicating that those with a conviction for disqualified driving are likely to be crime-versatile, with their offending more generalist and more reminiscent of mainstream offenders than simply a discrete category of driving offenders, albeit a serious driving offence (Roach, 2017). Driving while disqualified appears, therefore, to be another promising SSP tool for police to uncover versatile and serious criminality.

To rehearse the argument, a growing body of research evidence has shown that SSP promises to be a welcome addition to the police armoury for uncovering active, serious criminals, and with a greater 'offender hit rate', than, for example, randomly picking vehicle drivers (for example, Chenery et al, 1999; Maple, 1999; Townsley and Pease, 2003; Wellsmith and Guille, 2005; Roach 2007b).

The real beauty of SSP is that by virtue of the commission of a minor offence, our active, serious criminal makes him or herself (justifiably) eligible for official police attention. Wellsmith and Guille (2005) suggest that for SSP 'trigger offences' to be chosen they must fulfil three criteria:

- their acceptability in themselves for police attention;
- their empirical association with further and future criminality; and
- their unobtrusiveness in use since most of those targeted will not be active serious criminals.

Non-driving-related Self-Selection Policing examples

Although, admittedly, most of the SSP research to uncover minor 'trigger' offences to identify concurrent, serious criminality have been driver- and vehicle-related, the efficacy of other types of minor offence has (and are) been explored. Although not yet published, a recent study found that 'animal abuse' and 'animal cruelty' offences served as reliable SSP triggers of more serious criminality, especially violent crimes against humans.

Swindells, Roach, and Pease (2023, work in progress) are currently looking at the criminal records of those issued by police with an FPN for breaching 'lockdown' and 'social distancing' rules, in a certain area of Greater Manchester (UK) during the COVID-19 pandemic, as a means of identifying active, serious criminals.

Also related to the pandemic environment, I went for my COVID-19 vaccine 'booster' jab (injection) a few months ago, where I was told to sit in a large room for 15 minutes, before going home. Presumably, to check that I had no 'ill effects' from the vaccine. I was somewhat surprised that, from my random sample of 48 fellow 'recently vaccinateds', 15 walked straight through the waiting area and out the exit. Alas, before I could suggest exploring such 'non-compliance' as an SSP trigger offence for active, serious criminality, the UK government changed the 15-minute rule from compulsory to voluntary. You have to be fast in the SSP world – it's ever-shifting sands!

Now having presented some of the research and theoretical evidence to support it, why has SSP not been routinely adopted into UK police practice, and for that matter policing the world over? We now explore barriers and obstacles to its wider adoption by UK police, before suggesting how they might be overcome, so that SSP can be more fully incorporated into routine police thinking and practice.

Changing police psychology, policing policy, and police practice

In 2008 a UK Government-commissioned report 'The Review of Policing', the author, ex-police chief Sir Ronnie Flanagan, set out his recommendations for UK policing in the 21st century (Flanagan, 2008). Many of the report's final recommendations, unsurprisingly, set out how UK policing must change to combat serious and organised crime (including terrorism) and suggested that police resources needed to be 'freed up' in order to meet the challenges presented by serious criminals. Although most people (including me) will agree with Sir Ronnie's suggestion that serious crime should be a priority, what is most disappointing from an SSP perspective is how differentiated those who commit serious crimes and those who commit minor crimes were in the report. To mis-self-quote and say that 'those who do big bad things only do big bad things' would be the antithesis of the SSP approach and fly in the face of two decades of research by Ken Pease, myself, and others. At this, the highest policy level, there appeared at least to be little awareness or understanding of the bulk of the research on criminal careers and offending patterns, pointing to offence versatility. Without an appreciation that serious offenders also commit minor offences, then it is little surprise that the SSP approach has fallen largely on deaf ears with some high-level policymakers.

As previously alluded to, SSP challenges a common police misconception that serious offenders tend to specialise in the types of crime they commit, replacing it with the perception of serious offenders as exhibiting a high level of criminal versatility instead, that includes minor offences (Roach and Pease, 2013, 2016). To broaden police thinking towards placing attention on those who commit certain minor offences will therefore also focus attention on those who engage in active serious criminality. When specific minor offences are differentiated from all those possible, SSP can be used to uncover active, serious criminals.

Policy guidelines for police also set out criteria by which crimes should be screened prior to any investigation. Such a policy provides (1) a framework by which police are to initially assess whether a crime should be investigated further or not (known as 'filed first time'), (2) a crime seriousness and solvability guide, and (3) how officers and staff should be deployed to investigate a crime – commonly known as 'crime screening'. The crime screening decision-making processes, and the prioritisation of the crime for the allocation of resources for investigation, will depend on the category to which a crime is allotted.

What is of most interest to the adoption (or lack of) the SSP approach is that although serious and priority crimes are, and quite rightly, 'prioritised', minor 'non-priority offences' are totally disregarded unless there appears what are termed 'special aggravating features' (such as, repeat victimisation or evidence of victimisation). Crimes are therefore screened and then categorised in 'black and white', with serious and minor offenders constructed as homogenous and distinct groups. Such explicit crime-screening policy therefore also suggests a lack of awareness of the existence of links between serious offenders and minor offences, which again is at odds with SSP. The low priority given to most minor offences gets worse when 'solvability factors' are introduced into the screening process.

The operational justifications and policy reasons for crime screening are beyond the remit of this chapter and are merely mentioned here to illustrate the how deeply many policymakers continue to consider minor offences to be of such little importance. Indeed, most minor offences will fail to make it through the screening process, with only serious offences investigated and serious offenders targeted.

To summarise, although the research evidence and theoretical support for SSP is compelling (well at least I think so and I hope the reader is at least warming to the idea), it has not yet been widely incorporated into UK police practice. Indeed, more recently, Norwegian and American police have shown more interest. For SSP to become part of routine UK police practice, as an additional way by which police can identify active, serious criminals, then several changes and re-alignments have to be made.

First, as previously highlighted, a sea change in police thinking on criminal careers and offending patterns is required. When one understands that the main purpose of self-selection is to identify active *serious* offenders, then it no longer appears to clash with current police policy. When being sold to police, SSP must appeal to the serious crime agenda. As discussed, possibly the largest obstacle to self-selection is the police mindset, with the tendency to overestimate offence homogeneity. If, as anticipated, it is universal (Roach and Pease, 2013), then it must be breached before self-selection can be accepted. In my opinion, this will only be achieved with more research evidence to demonstrate offence heterogeneity, and if officers (particularly new recruits) are educated otherwise, possibly facilitated by the College of Policing[2] (now responsible for developing police doctrine and practice for England and Wales). To stress again, the incentive for change must be led by good-quality, evidence-based SSP research.

With regard to the wider topic of offender self-selection, acknowledgement must be given that many experienced and astute police officers already have an intuitive sense of the potential of offender self-selection. However, the argument here is as follows:

1. The minor offences that are chosen to trigger special attention should be based on research establishing the extent and nature of links with more serious offending. This removes subjectivity from the enforcement process.
2. A process should be established whereby the intuitions of police officers are made external and available, and tested against the evidence.

In short, SSP is not as much about rediscovering one aspect of the craft of policing, as it is about evidencing and quantifying links between offences of which some experienced officers have a sense and discarding those police intuitions which are unfounded.

The second suggestion involves a sea change in approach but links to the first. Despite the growing amount of criminological research suggesting that offenders (including serious) tend to be offence heterogeneous – particularly the criminal careers literature (for example, Farrington and Hawkins, 1991; Soothill et al, 2000; Farrington et al, 2006) – little attention is paid generally by criminologists to the possible significance of minor offences. As discussed, criminal career research neglects the importance of minor offences in a career, preferring to treat minor offences as markers of onset and evidence of de-escalation of seriousness, temporary or otherwise.

It is hoped that with the development of a growing body of research dedicated to self-selection this situation will change. In a spirit of encouragement, Table 5.1 provides a checklist to help the motivated reader

Table 5.1: Self-Selection Policing checklist

Minor offence criteria	Yes	No
Is it an actual offence? (for example, illegal parking)		
Does it justify enforcement in its own right? (for example, driving without a seat-belt)		
Is it evident by observation rather than detection? (that is, can someone committing it be easily seen doing it?)		
Will it take additional resources and if so what and how much? (that is, does it require more police time, money etc?)		
Is it unobtrusive to the public? (for example, will those found committing the offence be blissfully unaware of further background checks being done?)		
Will those identified committing it be investigated? (that is, can you ensure that those committing the offence will be scrutinised by police colleagues?)		
Can the offence also be identified by non-police agencies? (that is, can traffic wardens, parking attendants, and security guards also notice those committing the offence?)		
Is there a firm plan to evaluate this trial or study? If so, how?		
If found to be a successful SSP trigger, will its wider implication be met with resistance? If so, where? (for example, will a change in thinking or police culture be needed?)		
Do you plan to disseminate your findings widely and if so, how? (for example, articles, conference papers, police professional, and so on)		

Source: Reproduced from Roach and Pease, 2016

to think about and prepare to conduct an SSP trial. If you do, then please do share your thoughts and findings with me.

And finally

In a recent conversation with a police officer about the use of SSP he suggested that SSP is sometimes used as a way of targeting known criminals; for example, damaging a rear (tail) light so that questions and police scrutiny can be levied at an already known or suspected criminal. This is not SSP. SSP is an approach by which active, serious criminals are identified by certain minor offences that they freely commit, not by use of minor offences against known criminals and suspects to 'see what they are up to'. SSP is not an excuse for harassment. Tax evasion was not the SSP trigger offence which uncovered notorious gangster Al Capone as law-enforcement knew exactly who he was previously; rather, it was the offence for which he was charged when he eluded charges of more serious crimes.

Chapter summary

It has been shown that such a shift in common police psychology can afford valuable opportunities to identify active, serious criminals from the more minor offences that they commit (and commit more frequently). This change in police thinking has led to a corresponding change in police practice known as the 'Self-Selection Policing' approach (for example, Roach, 2007; Roach and Pease, 2016) of which numerous examples were presented.

Further reading

Chenery, S., Henshaw, C., and Pease, K. (1999) *Illegal Parking in Disabled Bays: A Means of Offender Targeting, Policing and Reducing Crime Briefing Note 1/99*, London: Home Office.

Roach, J. (2017) 'Self-Selection Policing and the disqualified driver', *Policing: A Journal of Policy and Practice*, 13(3): 300–11.

Roach, J. and Pease, K. (2016) *Self-Selection Policing: Theory, Research and Practice*, Basingstoke: Palgrave Macmillan.

Suggested resources

Episode number 44 of the Reducing Crime Podcast by Jerry Radcliffe: https://www.reducingcrime.com/podcast

University College London, Jill Dando Institute, Special Series on COVID-19, number 20: https://www.ucl.ac.uk/jill-dando-institute/sites/jill-dando-institute/files/self_selection_final_no_20.pdf

6

Psychology, expertise, and improving police officer street-craft

Introduction

In the Introduction to this book, it was stated that one of its primary aims was to help improve the transfer of 'tacit knowledge' (the knowing 'how to' do something and not just 'what to' do) between those working in policing, particularly from one generation of officer (or staff) to another. Indeed, I have already suggested that the guides and training available to new and inexperienced police officers overwhelmingly provide know-how on processes and procedures; for example, the 'Core Investigative Doctrine' (ACPO/Centrex, 2005), which, although providing valuable guidance on the basic processes and procedures of criminal investigation, says little about how to make good decisions and how to do things well, in the way that learned experience and a good mentor can (but not always) provide.

In this chapter, the concern for tacit knowledge transfer between police officers (and staff) is addressed to some degree, with a little added psychological understanding and knowledge, to suggest how frontline, routine, 'beat' policing, or what is affectionately referred to by many police officers 'longer in the tooth', as officer 'street-craft', can be improved, and the tacit knowledge hole plugged. More specifically, how the core duties of policing; that is, those high on the list of original '*Peelian principles*',[1] including the 'number one' to prevent crime (and others such as patrolling and dealing with the public) can be improved. By way of an example of how psychological research and police practice can work together, research is presented that mixes some basic knowledge of the psychology of lying and deceit with a common policing situation – that of asking individuals stopped by police their current address, before then moving to explore how psychology can explain some of the gems of tacit knowledge, referred to by some as 'police street-craft', that I have been lucky enough to pick up from 15 years of speaking with, working with, and observing police officers in action.

We begin the chapter with a brief exploration of what 'expertise' is and what it means to be 'an expert' and ask whether there is any specific psychology that lies behind (or underneath) them, which can be spread wider to all those involved in policing. It is important when distinguishing to what degree becoming an expert at something represents the end of (or at least a substantial way along) a learning process (for example, experience and practice), an 'acquired psychology' if you will, or whether it is innate (for example, in the genes) that you either have or do not have. Many policing and criminology students will, for example, be familiar with the 'offender profiling' literature written by ex-agents of the FBI from the 1980s and 90s, such as Robert Ressler (discussed previously in Chapter 2). Arguably the overriding impression promoted in the numerous often 'autobiographical accounts' of hunts for American serial killers was that offender profiling was more art than science, more about the innate skill of the agent, rather than the product or outcome of applying a sound scientific method. Personally, I took the message to be, 'Do not bother trying to be an offender profiler if you are not born with the necessary skills to do it'. The expertise of being an effective profiler was therefore described as being more attributable to the art and traits of the individual rather than the FBI profiling method, which at best was loosely based on a curious interpretation of personality psychology. I believed that this approach was at best naive and I still do to this day. Nobody is born to be an offender profiler. I accept that there might be certain characteristics and personal traits which if possessed can assist those learning to be offender profilers, in the same way that having long legs has helped Usain Bolt become the fastest man on the planet, but profiling expertise, like any other expertise, is mostly attributable to learning, knowledge, and experience, with far more experts made than are born. Having long legs alone did not make Usain Bolt superfast.[2] What exactly is an expert and how does someone become one, and more importantly for some readers perhaps, how can someone become an expert police officer? Presuming that there is such a person, of course.

Experts and their expertise

> When someone has gained special skills or knowledge representing mastery of a particular subject through experience and instruction, we call this person an expert. As experts are often able to perform well beyond the level of that less skilled people ordinarily attain or even think that they could ever attain, experts have been viewed as mysterious and are sometimes revered, much like those considered to be geniuses. (Ericsson, 2006a)

If somebody is classed as an expert, then what does that mean exactly? Alvin Goldman of Rutgers University, New Jersey, suggests that at least two conditions are necessary: 'One type of condition would pertain to the person's knowledge or information, and the other to his/her skill or performance ability' (2016, p 3).

Unfortunately, whatever experts are, or constitute, is not always looked on favourably as one still very prominent Conservative minister wrote not long ago in a UK newspaper, 'I think people in this country have had enough of experts' (Michael Gove, *The Telegraph*, 10 June 2016).[3]

As I write this chapter the world is battling the COVID-19 pandemic with the UK three weeks into a lockdown where social distancing and staying at home have been enshrined in law in order to help kerb the spread of the Coronavirus that has claimed over 9,000 lives in the UK up to today (10 April 2020). With the UK Government having followed the advice of experts, including prominent scientists (for example, virologists), one presumes that the now Cabinet Minister, Michael Gove, no longer sees experts as the enemy. Well, those scientists leading the fight against COVID-19 and who came up with a vaccine, anyway.

Most, however, believe 'expertise' to be a complimentary rather than pejorative term, with experts essential to solving difficult problems in the societies in which they live. What then *makes* someone an expert? Goldman provides quite a formulaic answer to this:

> S is an expert in domain D if and only if S has the capacity to help others (especially laypersons) solve a variety of problems in D or execute an assortment of tasks in D which the latter would not be able to solve or execute on their own. S can provide such help by imparting to the layperson (or other client) his/her distinctive knowledge or skills. (2016, p 4)

Philosophical debate about what, or what not, expertise and experts are, though masterly provided by Goldman (2016) is beyond the needs of this chapter. Suffice to say that simply experts 'help' in some way; for example, to solve problems that would ordinarily not be solved by someone without such expertise. Indeed, we shall leave the last word on this to Ericsson who suggests that expertise can be understood as a socially recognised characteristic linked to knowledge, technique, skills, or a combination of them all, which distinguishes someone from novices and less experienced people within a discipline (Ericsson, 2006b).

To date, research conducted in various different fields of decision-making has consistently shown that experts approach, think, and solve problems in different ways when compared with novices or the inexperienced (for example, see Ross, Shafer, & Klein, 2006). Experts, for example, tend to demonstrate better perceptual skills (Klein & Hoffmann, 1993) and richer schemata or 'stored knowledge' (Rouse & Morris, 1986), and possess greater tacit or 'how to do' knowledge in specific areas (for example, see Crandall, Kyne, Miltello, & Klein, 1992). Experts have been commonly found to devote proportionately more time to determining how to represent a problem but spend proportionately less time in executing solutions (Ross, Battaglia, Phillips, Domeshek, & Lussier, 2003 cited by Fahsing and Ask, 2016). From a psychological perspective, experts have been shown not only to be faster and more efficient in their decision-making, but also in how decisions are arrived at.

Expertise and policing

The reader may be justified in asking what good is any of this knowledge and research to those working in policing? The short answer is that by understanding how those with particular expertise have become 'experts', then we will be better placed to broaden the skills and knowledge bases of many more. A central question begged in this book is how can we expedite such a learning process? We shall return to criminal investigation, an area of UK policing which has become more 'professionalised' (Stelfox, 2008) and, as previously suggested, 'more expert' over the past two decades, in order to help provide answers to this question.

Criminal investigators as 'experts'

One area of psychological research that has focused directly on an aspect of policing is that of investigative decision-making, with some scholars focusing specifically on whether (and if so how) police investigators can become 'expert detectives' (Fahsing and Ask, 2016). Those of us partial to a crime mystery novel or a police drama series (now often referred to as a 'box set') can be forgiven for thinking that expert detectives, like Agatha Christie's *Hercule Poirot* or *Miss Marple*, or indeed Arthur Conan Doyle's *Sherlock Holmes*, were fictional figures gifted with amazing magical powers of deduction, induction, and logic. An interesting aside is how these famous fictional detective novels set in the late 19th and early 20th centuries, have all three characters as 'civilians' and not as police officers. Sherlock Holmes, for example, refers to himself as a 'consulting detective', possibly fostering an impression that their creators, at least, felt that investigative expertise was best coming from 'outsiders' than from police at the time. Indeed, all three of these fictional detectives serve to 'bail out' their police counterparts time and time again by solving the crimes that they could not have alone. Substitute crime fiction novels for more contemporary crime drama series and it is common for the main police detective character, such as *Jane Tennyson* in Linda La Plante's 'Prime Suspect',[4] or Peter Falk as *Columbo*[5] in the hit 1970s cop show, to be presented as 'flawed individuals', that often display 'clown-like' or sociopathic tendencies, or else have alcohol problems (or both) but are brilliant at the one thing that matters to those watching the dramas – solving crime mysteries. An overwhelming percentage of fictional depictions of expert detectives, therefore, tend less to portray them as the product of acquired expertise through experience and knowledge, and more as the possessors of some magical powers, a rare personality trait, or an ability which sets them above 'normal cops', as investigative experts.

Mercifully, with regard to contemporary UK policing, the fictional presentations do not mirror the reality anymore, and if it indeed ever did, then it was more a presentation of 1960s and 1970s detectives (for example, see Donnelly and West, 2018; or Hobbs, 1998 for a fuller account of UK detectives in this period). As I attempted to show earlier – experts tend to be made and not born. After all, even those considered to be naturally gifted at playing the piano need to learn, gain experience, endlessly practise, and (as a nod to my 'crime as opportunity'-thinking colleagues) have access to a piano.

In a seminal UK policing-based study, 'The effective Detective: identifying the skills of an effective Senior Investigating Officer', the authors, Smith and Flanagan (2000), found that the 'effective SIO depends upon a combination of management skills, investigative ability, and relevant knowledge, across the entire investigative process, from initial crime scene assessment through to post-charge case management' (2000, p 5*)*.

Although Ivar Fahsing, an academic researcher, and serving Detective Chief Superintendent with the Norwegian Police, suggests that investigative, or detective, expertise is formed through various experiences, practical guidelines, formal training, certification procedures, and on-the-job experience, it is still unclear whether these are all equally beneficial (Fahsing and Ask, 2016). In their study of detective/investigative decision-making, Fahsing and Ask (2016) found that the more experienced detectives in their sample were able to generate more alternative explanations and investigative actions than their less experienced counterparts. Interestingly, although professional experience may have improved the ability to generate and test investigative hypotheses in their UK sample of detectives, this was not found in the Norwegian sample of detectives. This, they suggest, is because they do not receive the same training and guidance as their UK counterparts, for whom it is compulsory to register on the Professionalising Investigative Practice Programme (for example, see Stelfox, 2008; James and Mills, 2012) and have the luxury of guides, such as the *Murder Investigation Manual* (ACPO, 2006) produced for SIOs, leading murder investigations. Further research has suggested that detectives must generate an adequate number of relevant investigative hypotheses (that is, what to investigate) and investigative actions (that is, how to investigate) (Fahsing and Ask, 2016; Fahsing, 2018) essential to the successful outcome of a criminal investigations and can reduce the risk of bias (for example, see Macquet, 2009; Simon, 2012; Alison et al, 2013). These findings suggest that expertise (namely, experience) generally improves the quality of investigative decision-making by those considered to be 'expert detectives' (Fahsing and Ask, 2016; Fahsing, 2018).

Learning from 'police expertise'

Several years ago, I was fortunate to be out socially with a couple of UK detectives that I had been working with, when one started talking about an ex-colleague of his who had been an 'ace thief-taker' in his day. I remembered having heard this phrase in 1970s cop shows, like 'The Sweeney',[6] but when I asked what he meant exactly, he said that this cop had been the best he'd known at spotting 'wrong uns'; that is, those up to no good (or about to be) before other officers did or did not. Indeed, the said officer could almost magically spot a criminal in a crowd of people. Like with Mr D in the Introduction to this book, I doubted that this man possessed magical powers and that the application of a little basic psychological understanding would explain this ability. More importantly, if I could find evidence to support my hypothesis that our 'ace thief-taker' was relying on certain observational and behavioural cues to identify those intent on 'no good', then this knowledge could be passed on to other, if not all, police officers and staff to use.

In an unpublished study, conducted between 2015 and 2016, I conducted ten interviews with nominated 'ace thief-takers' from four different UK police forces. All except one were of Police Constable rank (the other was a Police Sergeant) and all were male. Admittedly, as only a small sample size then only limited conclusions could be drawn, those interviewed had several things in common: (1) they all had excellent memories for faces and names; (2) they were all prepared to ask people questions if they had aroused their suspicions; (3) they all stated that they were always very polite when stopping an individual; (4) they were all prepared to be wrong about their suspicions and offer an apology afterwards; and (5) they were all enthusiastic about their work (particularly patrolling) even if their suspicions were aroused while not working (for example, while off duty and in a supermarket). Although this is not the most evidence-based, or indeed the most scientific study in the world, the findings are sufficient to suggest that being an 'ace thief-taker' (that is, having expertise in identifying criminals) is better explained by studying their learning about suspicious behaviour and why they are prepared to be wrong where others are not, than possessing any superpowers (innate or otherwise). Their 'expertise' was therefore not only explainable, but also potentially transferable to other police officers.

Psychology and enhancing police street-craft

Chapter 2 saw a brief discussion of the relationship between psychological research and policing, whereby a major contribution by the former to the practice of the latter was demonstrated in the detection of lies and deception.

Much of this research, however, relates to the findings in experimental conditions (often referred to as traditional psychological research), such as using scenarios in laboratories with students (that is, non-offenders) rather than in situ with police officers in real-life policing situations and contexts.

Although the value of applying psychological research and knowledge generated in laboratories is not disputed here, a common criticism is that it tends to lack any 'ecological validity'; that is, how it is implemented, performs, or operates in the 'real world'.

Unsurprisingly, suspect interview techniques tend to be developed for questioning arrestees in relatively time-rich situations (for example, conducted in police station interview rooms under police caution) but many more routine police–public interactions – for example, when on patrol – have a much smaller window within which police must establish the veracity of members of the public. For example, the truthfulness of answers to simple questions, such as what is an individual's name, address, and date of birth.

The next section of this chapter demonstrates how psychology might be applied in real time, such as how police decision-making in more 'time-poor' situations can be better understood and enhanced. Some of the research presented stems from my own observations of police officers making decisions in routine situations, such as when I observed two police officers ask a couple of young lads (messing about with a traffic cone on a street) their names and addresses. Although I couldn't hear exactly what was said, my police colleagues seemed happy with the responses that they had been given. Being naturally inquisitive (other descriptive verbs are available, of course) I asked how sure they were that the lads had furnished them with their real names and addresses. Both officers said that although they had not seen any documentary proof, they had been satisfied that they had been telling them the truth. Although to this day I do not doubt that my officer friends were indeed correct (well obviously a bit of me does or I wouldn't have researched it) it got me thinking about how easy it is to generate a false address within a very short space of time. A full address – that is, which includes a postcode (zip code to our American cousins). After all, police alarm bells would have rung if these young men had taken an aeon to respond to the simple question 'what are your names and addresses?' More importantly, I wondered whether those of us that can do this relatively easily are relying more on memory (that is, stored pre-existing knowledge and experience) rather than being expert at generating a seemingly random set of street names and numbers. I decided to conduct a simple quasi-experiment. The first common scenario that played over in my mind was to explore how easily people could generate a full false address (including a postcode).

Example 1: identifying false-address givers

Box 6.1 outlines the method used for this quasi-experiment with 142 undergraduate psychology students.

Box 6.1: A study of the psychology of false-address giving

All participants were given the following scenario:

You are stopped by police and asked for your address. You do not want them to know your real address. You have 15 seconds to come up with a false address including postcode.

Next they were asked to do the following:

1. Please write down your false address (including postcode).
2. Please see if you can make sense of how that false address was generated (for example, random address, similar to that of someone you know, an old address of yours, and so on) and if so write it down.
3. Please write down your real current address or that of where you consider to be your home address.

All response sheets were then collated and analysed using SPSS version 6.

Source: Roach, 2010

On completing the task, the data were collated and analysed. 75 per cent were female (n = 106), with an average age of 22 years (range 18–55 years, standard deviation of 6.3 years). All 142 students managed to generate a false address, which included a false postcode within the 15 seconds permitted (which was more generous than would be expected in a police–public interaction).

In terms of participants self-identifying the different thought processes that they had used to generate the false address, only 20 per cent believed this to be totally random. On closer inspection, however, some of these so-called 'random answers' were actually rather ridiculous, and one hopes would immediately raise the suspicions of the most moderately discerning police officer (for example, '666 Hell Lane'). The remaining seven categories stated appeared to have been generated from what cognitive psychologists refer to as 'top-down processing';[7] that is, pre-stored information retrieved from memory, such as a previous address, that of a known other, their real postal code (zip code), previous postal code, or the same address as theirs but a different house number.

Although at face-value the methods employed to generate false addresses by the participants appeared to be effective, on closer inspection our police officer would have stood a decent chance of tracking them down later, as all of them had unwittingly given some clues as to their real addresses, albeit to differing degrees. One presumes that those who gave the same address, but different number, would be easiest to trace with a bit of 'door-knocking', and that those who gave an old address' previous postcode, or the address of a 'known other' would be the next most easy to trace.

The learning from this brief experiment for policing practice was that participants appeared to find false-address generation difficult, as they overwhelmingly leaked true information 'clues' which could be used to (1) uncover their lying about their address, and (2) retrospectively, should police wish to trace a stopped person found to have given a false address, clues were given. The parallels with other techniques for identifying lies and deception (for example, the Guilty Knowledge Test discussed in Chapter 2) being obvious.

Of the 35 per cent of participants that gave a similar (but suitably different) postcode to their own and 'mixed' the numbers and addresses of known others would appear the most difficult for police to identify as either being liars face to face or, indeed, be able trace the whereabouts of afterwards. The details and findings of the false-postcode analysis, however, indicated that although some are better than others at generating a false address, most could not generate a false postcode that existed (see Box 6.2).

Box 6.2: Analysis of those who generated false postcodes in the psychology of false-address-generation study

- 96 per cent of participants gave a false postcode.
- Almost 70 per cent of false postcodes generated were found not to exist. Large majority of FPs looked bona fide but were not.

Cross-tabular analysis of generation false existing postcodes generation (FEP) (that is, those who managed to generate a false postcode that existed) showed:

- 96 per cent of participants could identify the thought process involved in the false existing.
- All relied heavily on TDP (15 per cent old address: 31 per cent known other, 22 per cent same/similar postcode).
- Females relied more than males on top-down processing to generate false existing postcodes.
- FEP from same town mean distance = 1.8 km (range = 0–12 km, SD = 2.9km).
- FEP from different town mean distance 55.6 km (range = 8.5 km, SD = 312 km).

However, these were twice as likely to be postcode of known other, than the sample.

The takeaway advice for police is, therefore, when they stop people on the street and ask them for their full address, to have immediate access to a postcode directory (for example, as a phone application), by which they can first verify that the postcode which an individual gives exists, and second, check that it corresponds to the full address that the individual has given them. If the postcode given is found either to not exist or to not to match the full address given, then the officer is wholly justified in asking more questions and to scrutinise the individual in front of them.

Put in SSP terms, by lying, the individual is more likely to be lying to conceal their concurrent, more serious criminality. Why else would you lie about your address? If you don't know your own postcode then why not just say so? Like the refusal to comply with a HO/RT1 or parking in an accessible parking bay illegally when other bays are available, it is the compulsion to lie which can be their undoing, but only if our diligent police officer is aware of the psychology of false-address generation.

Example 2: how to spot those lying about their date of birth

Feeling rather smug after conducting the psychology of false-address-generation study, I told a police officer friend of mine all about it. He immediately dampened my smugness by saying that he used to ask people for their postcodes many years ago while a police constable in Lancashire. Although I had an immediate thought that the Nobel Peace Prize would not be mine and that my world and career had ended,[8] I soon realised that this verified the value of my findings and that the police friend in question was not representative of all police officers, as most that I have asked since are not aware of this approach to uncovering false-address givers. Indeed, the police officer in question also told me how he used to scrutinise a date of birth given to him by a member of the public that he had stopped. Particularly, those that looked under the legal age for consuming alcohol at pubs, bars, and nightclubs. Like the postcode question, he would ask them their date of birth and then very quickly for their zodiac sign. He would then verify the sign given by checking it with a list of zodiac signs that he had cut from a women's magazine (see Box 6.3). In the space of five minutes he had gone from heartbreaker to genius, and I decided to test his approach.[9]

Adopting an approach very similar to that used in the psychology of false-address generation study, student participants were given a scenario in which they were to devise a false date of birth (shown in Box 6.4).

From a sample of 129 students, 77 per cent reported identifying as female (n = 99). A total of 65 per cent said that they could identify where the false date of birth that they had generated had come from, with 35 per cent saying that it was random.

Box 6.3: The signs of the zodiac

Capricorn	22 December – 19 January
Aquarius	20 January – 18 February
Pisces	19 February – 20 March
Aries	21 March 21st – 19 April
Taurus	20 April – 20 May
Gemini	21 May – 20 June
Cancer	21 June – 22 July
Leo	23 July – 22 August
Virgo	23 August – 22 September
Libra	23 September – 22 October
Scorpio	23 October – 21 November
Sagittarius	22 November – 21 December

Box 6.4: A study of the psychology behind false dates of birth

129 psychology student participants took part in a 'false date-of-birth generation' quasi-experiment. They were given the following scenario:

You are stopped by police and asked for your date of birth. You do not want them to know your real date of birth. You have 15 seconds to come up with a false date of birth and the corresponding zodiac sign.

Participants were asked next to record their actual date of birth and zodiac sign to afford comparisons with the false one they had provided.

Finally, participants were asked to attempt to explain why they think that generated the false date of birth they provided (for example, whether it was random, a family member's, like their own, or a friend's).

Source: Roach, Pease, and Clegg, 2011

47 per cent had given a zodiac sign that did not correspond to the false date of birth they gave. The findings of T-tests suggested that age and gender did not appear to influence the correct matching of zodiac sign to false date of birth.

Indeed, 37 per cent said that they did not have a clue and just gave a random zodiac sign to accompany the false date of birth. Those who got a correctly corresponding zodiac sign and false date of birth match stated that they knew it was the correct sign for the false date of birth given, because both were those of a relative or close friend. Top-down processing in action once more.

My policeman colleague, when on patrol in the 1980s, appeared to have used a reliable way of identifying false dates of birth when asking people for their zodiac signs. With the psychology of doing so rather promising, then the takeaway advice for all police on patrol who ask people their date of birth should also ask them for their zodiac sign, and then check (via Google perhaps?) to see if date and sign match. If they do not, then further scrutiny of the individual is both warranted and justified. As with the false-address generation study, why would you lie about your zodiac sign unless you were lying about your date of birth? And if so, what else might you be lying about? As with both the lying about your address and age studies, if an individual says that they do not know their postcode or zodiac sign, then this approach is dead in the water. It, therefore, relies upon the ego of those wanting to hide their personal details from police, by instinctively wanting to lie themselves out of a situation, rather than simply claiming ignorance. Further research is welcome in this area.

Chapter summary

Hopefully, this brief chapter serves to illustrate how bringing together a little psychological understanding with some policing expertise can be used to advance routine police practice for all police officers. Like many of the other chapters in this book, it represents merely a start of thinking about how to improve police practice, in this case enhancing police 'street-craft', rather than a definitive guide.

Further reading

Fahsing, I. and Ask, K. (2016) 'The making of an expert detective: the role of experience in English and Norwegian police officers' investigative decision-making', *Psychology, Crime & Law*, 22(3): 203–23.

Roach, J. (2010) 'Home is where the heart lies? A study of false address giving to police', *Legal and Criminological Psychology*, 15(2): 209–20.

Roach, J., Pease, K., and Clegg, K. (2011) 'Stars in their lies: how better to identify people who give false dates of birth to police', *Policing: A Journal of Policy and Practice*, 5(1): 56–64.

Suggested resources

The Crime Prevention Website: https://thecrimepreventionwebsite.com/ (accessed 24 January 2022)

7

Psychology and crime prevention

Introduction

With this chapter we explore how psychological knowledge and research can be used to inform policing, by helping to reduce the chances of a crime happening in the first place. Unlike criminology, crime prevention is of course not concerned primarily with targeting those who would commit crime, but with working to reduce the number of potential victims of crime by encouraging people to be more security conscious where they are currently not (for example, by routinely locking doors and windows in their home when they are absent) and by identifying places that appear to act as 'attractors' of criminal behaviour and modifying them (for example, dark alleyways and badly run pubs).

We concentrate our focus therefore on how psychology can inform policing in what Brantingham and Faust (1976) refer to as 'primary crime prevention' (1976) and not on what they refer to as 'tertiary crime prevention' which is preventing known individuals from re-offending; for example, police targeting of organised crime groups (OCGs) or those being released from prisons.

The psychology of preventing crime

The three levels of crime prevention

Brantingham and Faust (1976) identify three levels of crime prevention: *primary level*, whereby prevention is directed at modification of criminogenic conditions in the physical and social environment; *secondary*, by focusing on those deemed at risk of becoming offenders; and *tertiary*, the targeting of 'known criminals' to prevent them from committing crime (Brantingham and Faust, 1976). As discussed in a previous chapter, Situational Crime Prevention (SCP) is firmly rooted at the 'primary' prevention level as it is concerned with reducing crime by employing modifying environments in ways that deter anybody from crime and not just those who are already active offenders. It is to SCP that we now turn our attention, particularly the psychology behind this approach to preventing crime.

Situational Crime Prevention

SCP (Clarke, 1983) is principally concerned with developing and promoting practical measures to prevent a crime, by focusing on reducing the specific opportunities for it. This is primarily achieved through manipulations of immediate environments in which a crime occurs (Hodgkinson and Farrell, 2017). For example, the fitting of alarms and immobilisers as standard on new cars by their manufacturers saw an immediate and significant reduction in the number of new cars stolen in the UK essentially because the act of stealing a new car became harder (Farrell and Brown, 2016).

The psychology behind SCP is simple – to manipulate and moderate environments in ways that reduce opportunities to commit crime. Dark alleyways are obvious places for crimes to happen by virtual of them being dark alleyways. According to SCP thinking, make dark alleyways not dark alleyways anymore, and then opportunities to commit crime in them – for example, street robbery or drug dealing – will reduce as those who would use them for crime will likely be deterred due to a perceived increase in the chances of being seen/getting caught. Not all will be deterred in this example, of course, but with a significant number likely to be, many crimes can be prevented. As mentioned in an earlier chapter, SCP rests on several proven theories: Cohen and Felson's Routine Activity Theory (RAT) (1979) and Cornish and Clarke's Rational Choice Theory (RCT) (1985).

To recapitulate, RAT explains how offenders come across 'crime opportunities', more in the course of doing their 'routine activities' or as they go about their daily business; for example, a motivated offender walking past a car with an open car window and a handbag on the front seat is likely to see it as an opportunity to commit theft, rather than going to the effort of deliberately searching for such a golden opportunity. As SCP is concerned with reducing specific opportunities for crime, RAT is important because it identifies three essential ingredients for any crime opportunity: a *suitable target* (that is, person, place or thing), a *motivated offender* (that is, an individual who can first recognise and second act upon a crime opportunity), and the *absence of a capable guardian* (that is, a lack of someone or something to stop an individual acting on a crime opportunity such as a security guard or passer-by) (see Felson, 1987). The psychology is obvious here – remove one of the three ingredients (for example, by closing the car window and removing the handbag), then that environment or situation ceases to be perceived by some as a crime opportunity.

RCT (Cornish and Clarke, 1979) is equally important in terms of providing theoretical support to SCP as it seeks to explain how offenders (or those who would) decide to act on crime opportunities as they present themselves. 'Rational' decision-making' in this sense is, for example, when an individual decides whether to act on a perceived opportunity, by weighing up the potential rewards gained (for example, money for selling stolen property) against the costs of committing the crime (for example, getting caught and going to prison). Rationality is assumed when our individual does not act on a perceived opportunity to commit the crime because the reward does not justify the risk.

Cornish and Clarke (2003) advance the SCP approach in developing a number of practical techniques for preventing crime which are based on the basic psychology of RAT and RCT, organised within five different categories of intervention to deter a would-be offender by*: increasing the effort* (for example, target hardening); *increasing the perceived risk* (for example, use of CCTV); *reducing the rewards* (for example, a valued item which ceases to function if removed illegally); *removing excuses* (for example, signage stating that illegal parking will result in wheel-clamping), and *removing provocation* (for example, not wearing the football shirt of your favourite football team in a pub frequented by rival fans).[1] All 25 techniques for preventing crime seek to influence a would-be offender's decision-making by modifying environments that are seen to facilitate crime (for example, a rowdy, overcrowded bar will most likely see tempers tested and regular fighting and violence at weekends) in ways that deter would-be offenders from acting on perceived criminal opportunities (for example, reducing the capacity of our currently overcrowded bar and ensuring that sufficient numbers of bar staff are on duty at weekends, to serve customers as quickly as possible).

Since its development in the 1980s, SCP has continued to inform many successful crime prevention interventions around the world and for many different types of crime. SCP-inspired burglary prevention initiatives continue to provide good examples, such as targeted use of CCTV, alley gating, hot-spot policing, street lighting, and Neighbourhood Watch, to name but few (for example, see Bennett et al, 2008; Welsh and Farrington, 2009; Sidebottom et al, 2017). Based on seven systematic reviews, David Weisburd and colleagues conclude that SCP interventions have proven overwhelmingly successful at preventing various types of crime but particularly those which are theft related (Weisburd et al, 2017). So how does SCP work exactly?

SCP techniques comprise manipulations of immediate environments in which a crime occurs, often imported from the natural world where, for example, animals evolve in ways which increase their protection against natural predators (for example, biomimetics). *Target hardening*, for example, often parallels the way evolutionary processes have shaped the natural defences of many 'preyed upon' species, whereby impenetrable shells, and thick skins (for example, rhinoceros) have evolved to protect prey from the claws and teeth of would-be predators (Roach and Pease, 2013). In an ever-changing evolutionary 'arms race', the flip side is that predators evolve to counter changes in their prey's security, so as over thousands of years gazelles have increased their speed, so have most of the big cats that prey on them (Roach and Pease, 2013). If not, then that way the extinction of a species lies.[2] Paul Ekblom draws our attention to the implications for crime prevention by highlighting how improvements in the strength and locks on safes led those determined to steal their contents to the use of oxyacetylene torches to 'crack' them open (Ekblom, 2000).[3]

Mimicking nature in many ways, the security of a property is often 'target hardened' to make its theft more of a challenge, more of a risk, and more effortful for would-be thieves; for example, by fitting a burglar alarm, putting security locks on doors and windows, or getting a big dog with a bad attitude towards strangers, thereby deterring them (in the short term at least) from burgling a particular property (Hirschfeld et al, 2010). Target hardening has been found to be an effective measure of crime prevention, particularly in relation to domestic burglary victimisation (Hirschfeld, 2004; Millie and Hough, 2004; Hamilton-Smith and Kent, 2005) and is often a popular means by which individuals can take basic precautions to protect themselves from criminal victimisation (for example, by ensuring that all doors and windows are shut and locked).

There is often a need for crime prevention measures to be employed swiftly and used appropriately if they are to be effective, and although SCP interventions continue to be a popular default position in trying to prevent crime, when humans are involved they can be ineffective; for example, when we forget (or refuse) to carry out even the most basic of security behaviours, such as locking doors and windows or setting an alarm before we leave the house. This renders even the most sophisticated of SCP techniques paralysed.

As we have seen, the SCP approach is often employed effectively to deter would-be offenders, by influencing their perceptions of criminal opportunities sufficiently enough to deter them from acting upon them. Indeed, as Felson and Clarke (1998) would have it, 'Opportunity makes the thief' . It does not, however, explain how opportunities for crime are recognised by a potential offender in the first place. In which case perhaps 'opportunity makes the theft more likely' is arguably nearer the mark. For example, an open upstairs window will appear to most of us (if indeed it is noticed at all) to be a way of letting in cool air into a house on a hot day, but to some it will represent a burglary opportunity. We need to visit some basic psychology on human perception if we wish to understand how criminal opportunities are realised and how crime might be prevented.

Affordance: the psychology of recognising a criminal opportunity?

At a risk of stating the obvious (which admittedly has never stopped me before) opportunities can only be realised if they are recognised as being so. I have an opportunity to win the lottery only if I decide to buy a ticket. I don't, because I do not see it as an opportunity for me to win millions of pounds. Others do, and good luck to them. In the criminal context, one can only exploit an opportunity for crime if one recognises that it is an opportunity to commit a crime. A thief looking to steal people's bags, mobile phones, and wallets is unlikely to visit a train station at 10 pm because the opportunities to steal will be somewhat limited compared with rush hour when the train station is full of bustling people, some of whom will be distracted with getting the next train and who may not be aware that their bag with their purse or wallet is wide open, or as I have noticed all too frequently lately, that their mobile phone is sticking up out of the rear pocket of their jeans. Most people will not see these as opportunities to steal, but those of a criminal persuasion are likely to. Situations and objects, therefore, can be missed or perceived in different ways and are generally only seen as criminal opportunities by those inclined to committing crime. This is known as 'affordance' (Gibson, 1966, 1975).

Put simply, affordance is what connects perception and action or perception of a criminal opportunity with criminal action. Affordance theory was developed by J.J. Gibson in 1966 and describes how we perceive our world not only in terms of object shapes and spatial relations but also as object–action possibilities or what we can do with that object (that is, affordances). That is, how we perceive of an object implies the action associated with it. Ken Pease gives the brilliant example of baseball bat sales and usage in the UK. Although thousands of bats are sold each year, by comparison very few baseballs are, strongly suggesting that in the UK only a small percentage of those who buy them use them to play baseball. The logical conclusion is that baseball bats for most 'afford' a different use other than that which they were designed, not for playing sport, but as weapons (Pease, 2006).

Affordance as a concept was popularised by the designer and psychologist Donald Norman (1998) who applied it to everyday objects and what they 'afford' us. Norman gives the example of a plate on a door which implies a 'push' (often we do this unconsciously) where a handle (usually found on the other side of the same door) instead encourages to engage in a 'pulling' action. I am living proof of how it can all go pear-shaped if this is reversed, as one of the doors in the building where I work has the handle on the 'pushing side' and the plate on the 'pulling side'. To say that this door does not get me every time and that it does not drive me mad when it does would be an understatement. So much so that I have asked the Estates people on several occasions over the years whether they know that that door defies the logic of affordance, but I always get the same answer – no!

Coming back to somewhere near crime prevention, Ken Pease has further applied the implications of the affordance concept to considerations of how one's perceived actions are constrained (or in some cases widened) by what one infers others might do in particular situations (Pease, 2006). For example, if one perceives a dog to be hostile, then the consequent range of possible actions available (that is, afforded) is likely to be more constrained than if it is perceived as friendly or harmless (Roach, 2012). Particularly, if that individual is surveying potential burglary targets. Having a guard dog may signify that something is worth stealing inside.

In an 'affordance-based' experiment, Roach, Alexander, and Pease (2012) found people to be all too ready and willing to make inferences about the reasons why a liveried police vehicle was present outside a dwelling. These inferences differed according to the type of dwelling type (for example, detached house, high-rise flat, or terraced house). Different dwelling types appeared to 'afford' different explanations for why police were attending. An overwhelming majority of participants stated that they thought that the police car parked was parked outside a high-rise block because police were there in a confrontational context (for example, to arrest someone living there), but not when the same police car was pictured parked outside a luxurious, detached house, where police were considered more likely to be there for supportive reasons (for example, to investigate a report of a burglary).

So why does affordance generated by the presence of a police car at a particular type of dwelling matter? The potentially troubling conclusion that Roach et al (2012) suggest is that, however reassuring the police visits are designed to be, for those merely seeing the police vehicle, cues can be taken from the setting which will determine the interpretation of the police presence. Speculatively, crime-challenged areas will yield most presumptions of confrontation; for example, that the police are there to arrest someone.

Put in a further criminal context, affordance can be taken to be simply the range of behaviours that individuals might consider if they perceive situations in particular ways (Pease, 2006). An obvious example is the 'Broken Windows' hypothesis (Wilson and Kelling, 1982; Kelling and Coles, 1995) founded on the observation that a rundown, damaged building (or bus shelter) is likely to afford criminal interest in a way that an undamaged one will not. The thinking being, that is that if people appear not to care about an area, then they won't care if criminals exploit it.

Along the same theme, seeing that someone has obviously committed a crime – for example, our already damaged vehicle – for some will be seen as almost permission to continue. The social psychologist Philip Zimbardo (1973, 2007) found in an experiment that the perception of a vehicle with a missing wheel afforded vandalism and theft opportunities that a complete vehicle did not. In relation to criminal affordance varying with the area in which the vehicle was left, Nee and Meenaghan (2006) found that those most experienced in burglary processed cognitively relevant stimuli and cues available from settings faster when searching for targets, suggesting 'expertise'.

These examples have led Pease to suggest (2006) that affordance may be thought of as the psychology which links a predisposition to a setting. In terms of crime prevention, what must be manipulated psychologically is the affordance of crime opportunities by those who perceive them. In my opinion, the best way of achieving this is 'from the horse's mouth' by asking them what to them affords good opportunities for different types of crime. This I was doing with incarcerated prolific car thieves until the COVID-19 pandemic made it easier to get out of a UK prison than to visit one.

In summary, the psychology of affordance is crucial to understanding how offenders recognise criminal opportunities, if SCP and other crime prevention approaches are to be effective. We now turn to our crime prevention attention to another psychological approach that is rather unflatteringly referred to as 'nudging' (Thaler and Sunstein, 2008).

Nudge: psychology to influence victims and potential victims of crime

Although the 'nudge' approach to influencing human choice-making was presented by Thaler and Sunstein in 2008, within a seemingly new way of looking at decision-making called 'behavioural economics', anybody who knows anything about psychology will tell you that it resembles more a repackaging (although much warranted) of the psychology of influence (for example, cognitive behaviourism) and not a brand-new approach. They state that human decision-making is susceptible to subtle 'nudges' that can encourage more prosocial behaviour. In their eponymous book *Nudge*, they demonstrate brilliantly how nudges can be employed effectively to encourage us all to behave more 'prosocially', such as increasing organ harvesting through increased donations, increasing pension saving, and increasing tax returns. Nudge, unsurprisingly, has been labelled by some as 'liberal paternalism', where those with the power decide what is best for us and encourage us to behave accordingly; for example, to give up smoking. Nevertheless, it continues to prove popular with many policymakers around the globe.

Thaler and Sunstein (2008) stress that nudges do not remove individual choice, but simply rearrange the choices available in such a way as to encourage uptake of the prosocial option. Rather like (albeit a crude example) presenting a list of options on a screen for an individual to choose from, but with one desired presumably by those providing the list, in bold typeface. The option being nudged, they argue, is the choice most of us would make in time, such as paying our taxes and not drinking too many fizzy drinks. Nudges are inherently simple and work on a rudimentary understanding of human decision-making processes and what influences us. As discussed previously in the chapter on decision making, according to eminent psychologists Daniel Kahneman and Amos Tversky (see Tversky and Kahneman, 1992; or see

Kahneman, 2011, for an excellent precis of their work), there are two basic systems of human decision-making: 'system one', which largely operates at the unconscious level, such as 'acting on instinct' or on our 'intuition', and 'system two', which requires concerted effort, thought, and calculation, and is sometimes referred to as deliberate or rational decision-making. There are some situations, of course, that necessitate quick system one thinking (for example, to run away from a dangerous situation) and some which require more depth of thinking (for example, which university should I choose, or indeed should I go to university at all). 'Nudging' essentially represents the employment of specific 'psychological prompts' designed to influence system one (unconscious thinking) by utilising numerous cognitive biases and heuristics (mental shortcuts). Roach et al (2016), for example, suggest that when a shop assistant says to you, "that will be just £1.99" when you purchase an item, which was the same price the day before, and will doubtless still be the day after, this represents a deliberate 'sales nudge' to get you to shop with them again. How? A deliberate use of the word 'just' is the nudge to our unconscious encouraging us to feel that we have got a good deal, a better deal than perhaps another shop would have given us, as the item is cheaper in this shop. If we think we have got a 'special deal' then we will be far more likely to shop there again. Our choice of where to shop has not been taken away, just the amplification of this shop in our future shopping-related decision-making. Apologies if you now feel that you have been had. Take comfort in the fact that you are far from being the only one – we all have been. Indeed, the familiar saying 'that you can only con a greedy man' is pertinent here as it suggests that 'greedy men' (or women) are more likely to be fraudulently parted from their money by the appeal of getting something cheaper or by cheating someone else. The point being made is that by using such nudges your choice of where to shop in the future is not being narrowed or constrained, just influenced (that is, nudged) very slightly to promote the shop in question. Now where is the harm in that?

Application of the nudge approach has expanded exponentially since its initial inception, with many governments employing nudges in numerous public campaigns, such as encouraging their citizens to live healthier lives; for example, exercising more and, of course, giving up smoking. In the UK, the Behavioural Insights Team (BIT), formally of the UK Cabinet Office, developed a checklist of influences on our behaviour for use when making policy, using the mnemonic MINDSPACE (MINDSPACE, 2010).[4]

Acronyms are, of course, themselves nudges, being themselves ways of facilitating decision-shaping ways of thinking. There is no shortage of acronyms or practice guides in the nudge literature, but MINDSPACE is a useful one if nudges are thought of as constituting simple and cheap measures that may be put in place and readily tested for their effects on decision-making, when compared with expensive situational measures, such as the installation of close-circuit television. The advantage of keeping it simple, at least in the crime reduction context, is that it is less likely to deter police and other agencies from being too cautious or committing the worst type of failure, which is inertia. When anti-crime nudges are cheap to implement, then one can afford to roll out lots of them and see which work in an 'evidence-based' way. So, has there been a tsunami of nudge-inspired interventions in crime prevention? No!

Although the use of nudges has become common in public policy initiatives and economic research, their use within crime prevention has lagged somewhat behind. To date, only a handful of published examples exist where the nudge approach has been employed to prevent crime. In one such study by Daniel Nettle and colleagues, a significant reduction in bicycle thefts from a university campus was achieved by displaying posters of 'watching eyes' placed close to 'hot-spot' bike-sheds (Nettle et al, 2012). Presumably, the 'watching eyes' nudged many of the potential bike thieves into feeling less confident and more uneasy about stealing bikes from these sheds because of the eyes made them feel more conspicuous, producing an uneasy feeling, based on the fact most of us don't like being watched. Visit any church in the UK and there will be pictures, statues, stained-glass windows, and other artefacts with people and 'things' looking at you, to remind us all that God is watching us and that we need to obey the rules. Maybe these particular bike thieves were nudged not to steal the bikes as the eyes held religious connotations for them, but we shall never know. Suffice to say, 'the eyes had it' (sorry).

Sharma and Kilgallon-Scott (2015) suggest that thefts from shops can be reduced when signs declaring that 'savings made from reductions in shop thefts will be donated to charity' are displayed, although they offer no direct empirical evidence to support this. This raises the important point that nudges only stand a chance of success if the individual is close to making the desired choice already. In this case, if they have a conscience. As many a police officer will testify, those most entrenched in criminal careers are not likely to make different choices (such as not to offend anymore) based on a nudge, subtle or otherwise. Ken Pease usefully describes the way nudges work as being like placing a small weight on one end of a finely balanced seesaw, just enough to tip it completely in one direction (not anything to do with the boy band of the same name) either up or down. If our 'decision see-saw' is not finely balanced in the first place, then the additional weight of a small nudge is unlikely to affect its overall balance. The moral of the analogy, in terms of preventing crime, being that pushes and shoves (metaphorical and otherwise) are far more likely to influence the decisions and choice-making of seasoned criminals than nudges. Which is often why a more appropriate use for nudges when trying to prevent crime is to encourage people to make choices that reduce their chances of becoming a victim of crime in the first place.

One such crime-victim-focused study, by Roach et al (2016), saw a 'nudge inspired' leaflet, developed for use by Durham Police to use in a known 'hot-spot area', for thefts from 'insecure' (that is, unlocked) vehicles. Theft from insecure vehicles in one area had been a particular problem with up to 25 per cent of all such thefts attributed to unlocked/left-open vehicles. A profile analysis of previous victims identified that the vehicle owners tended to be busy parents with young families who had forgotten to lock their vehicle(s) parked on their driveways overnight. They had forgotten to 'zap' (remotely lock) their vehicle.

Roach et al (2016) state that after speaking with some local residents (and indeed local thieves) it was decided that a bespoke, targeted leaflet drop was the most appropriate means by which to deliver a 'please check that you have locked your vehicle' message. The wording on the leaflet (that is, 'the message') was very much informed by knowledge of evolutionary psychology (the message appeals to the residents' paternal/maternal buttons by reference to making it 'easy' by leaving kids' gaming devices in the car), *nudge psychology*, and by the work of Kahneman et al (1982), particularly their finding of our intense dislike of having something or someone taken from us, known as 'loss aversion' (that is, hence use of the phrase don't 'make it easy for them').

Although analysis of the 'nudge target areas' suggested that posting leaflets through the letterboxes of residents would be the most likely means of delivering the message, the likely obstacle foreseen was that generally any leaflet posted through a letter box makes its way very quickly to a rubbish bin without being read at all. To help get the attention of the residents, the leaflets displayed a photograph of the street in which they lived. Although they do not state whether this tactic had a significant effect on the uptake of the message, logically it is safe to assume that nothing grabs our attention quite like a large dose of familiarity (that is, why is my street on this leaflet?)

The 'easy leaflets' distributed to increase the security-conscious behaviour of the residents in the target areas saw a significant reduction in the percentage of thefts from insecure vehicles, in the two 'treatment' areas by 9 per cent and 7 per cent, with no corresponding increase in the percentage of thefts from secure vehicles (Roach et al, 2016). So no discernible crime 'displacement effect'. Although few, the initial success of applying the nudge approach to preventing crime, especially encouraging vehicle owners in Durham to think and behave in a more security-conscious way (Roach et al, 2016), served to enthuse its further use to reduce student burglary victimisation in a high-risk area of Durham City, with significant success (see Roach et al, 2018).

In a spirit of helpfulness, Box 7.1 presents NUDGE-IT, a list of considerations for those thinking of developing crime-prevention-focused 'nudges'.

Box 7.1: NUDGE-IT

Nuanced – Nudges must be subtle and with testable hypotheses.

Unconscious – Nudges tap into existing bias and default decision-making.

Discerning – Nudges should target those on the cusp of choosing the prosocial option.

Give people a choice – Nudges provide choice but encourage uptake of one in particular.

Easy – Nudges must be easy to explain and implement.

Inexpensive – Nudges should be cheap to develop, implement, and modify.

Testable – Nudges require a robust evaluation framework to test their effectiveness.

We now move to the idea of 'repeat victimisation' and the psychology behind common explanations for it.

A psychology of repeat victimisation

Research on crime victimisation by Farrell and Pease found that in England and Wales, 4 per cent of the population suffer 44 per cent of crime suffered (for example, see 1993, 2001, 2017). Crime victimisation is therefore highly disproportionate, with a small number of people being repeatedly victimised. Whether one becomes a victim of crime or not appears to have little to do with chance or 'bad luck', with several identifiable characteristics making some more likely to become victims than others (Ainsworth, 2001).

What is the psychology behind this? Well for some crimes it is more obvious than for others; for example, where victims of domestic violence remain living with a violent partner, the chance of repeat victimisation is a readily identifiable as a 'high risk' situation. Much of the repeat victimisation research has tended to focus on burglary, in trying to work out why some residences are frequently targeted by criminals where others are not. A house may be repeatedly targeted for a variety of reasons; for example, research by Bennett (1995) found that if a house is targeted repeatedly, it may be because it almost gives off signals inviting intrusion. Referred to as the *flag* explanation (Pease, 1998; Tseloni and Pease, 2003), this is when something about it is akin to displaying a big flag with 'this house is conducive to burglary' written on it for all (including burglars) to see. These 'psychological signals' obviously need to be removed so that it is perceived to be a more formidable challenge, deterring instead those thinking of burgling it. 'Thus a house which was originally selected as a target because it had poor locks and was left unoccupied for long periods of time may become a much less attractive target if better locks are fitted, an alarm installed and a new occupant with a large dog moves in' (Ainsworth, 2001, p 56).

Pease (1998) suggests that a first offence educates the offender, serving to *boost* the chance of repeat victimisation because of additional familiarity with the layout of the house (for example, entrance and exit points), the likely rewards available, and makes them more confident because they 'got away with it' last time. Flag explanations of repeat victimisation, therefore, focus on the environment and situation (dwelling in the case of burglary), where boost explanations focus on the offender.

Knowledge of repeat victimisation facilitates more targeted crime prevention. If police and victims know who is likely to become a victim in the future, then more 'scatter-gun' approaches, often with little prospect of success, are minimised. This has led to a more predictive crime approach, especially for burglaries (for example, see Bowers et al, 2004).

In terms of the explaining the psychology behind repeat victimisation, the evidence suggests that those committing crimes against the same target are primarily the same offenders (for example, Bernasco, 2008); a second offence against the same target being overwhelmingly committed by the same offender that committed the first (for example, see Ashton et al, 1998). More support is provided by Matthews et al (2001) who found that such offenders tended to be the most prolific of criminals, with some perpetrating the same crime against the same victim dozens of times. Bernasco's research comes to the same conclusion (Bernasco, 2008). Understanding and utilising knowledge of repeat victims, therefore, allows police to better interpret patterns of crime and more chance of apprehending the most prolific offenders (Pease, 1998; Everson and Pease, 2001). Despite this, Pease et al claim that its use has for some reason declined with 'policy makers and implementers despite repeat victims accounting for increasing proportions of total crime' (2018, p 256).

We end this chapter with some practical psychology-based advice to help those charged with reducing and preventing crime deal with the accusation that encouraging people to be more conscious of opportunities for crime, such as targeting repeat victimisation, is actually 'blaming victims' for the crimes they experience.

Crime prevention and avoiding accusations of victim blaming

One of the commonly used sticks with which to beat crime prevention initiatives is that they blame the victims for the crimes that they endure. From personal experience, I have seen, on countless occasions, senior officers baulk at introducing crime prevention initiatives, often due to fear that their Force will be accused of 'victim blaming' if it uses messages that identify potential victims; for example, by pointing out that burglary is prevalent in an area because some residents are forgetting to lock their doors and windows when they leave their properties. As was hopefully demonstrated earlier in the chapter in relation to using 'nudges', the sentiment of the message may be noble (that is, we want you to reduce your chances of becoming a victim of crime) but its interpretation by others is very much dependent on the framing of the message and how it is delivered.

Let us apply a little psychology to understand better what might be happening here and how encouraging better awareness of personal security and risk might be more positively reframed.

Box 7.2: Locus of control and encouraging people to think about preventing crime

Locus of control is a personality construct relating to an individual's beliefs about the extent to which an individual feels in control of what happens to them and the extent to which they can affect their own life.

- Strong **external locus of control** is when someone believes what happens to them is luck or fate (that is, they are not in control of their life) all due to external forces in their environment (for example, live in a high-crime area).
- Strong **internal locus of control** is when someone believes they are in control of what happens to them (for example, with better security I can reduce my chances of being a victim).

Box 7.2 provides a brief introduction to 'locus of control' (Rotter, 1966), which is a personality construct in psychology relating to how much an individual believes that they have control over their own decisions and behaviours.

One way of helping police and others to spread crime prevention messages which encourage us to be more careful with our personal security (for example, not going to remote areas alone at night) and our personal possessions (for example, not leaving valuables on display in our cars) is to 'nudge' a small shift in some people's perceptions of from one of a strong external locus of control (for example, it doesn't matter what I do because I live in a high-crime area) to a stronger internal locus of control (for example, if I remember to lock the car then I am making it harder to steal).

Such a psychological move an individual's sense of control affords opportunities to reframe crime prevention as 'empowering people' to protect themselves as opposed to simply blaming victims for their actions ('victim blaming').

Here are five suggested ways to minimise accusations of victim blaming for crime prevention initiatives/interventions aimed at potential victims (not an exhaustive list and in no particular order) using the REACT acronym (see Box 7.3). I am using 'potential victims' as short-hand for those being selected for a specific crime prevention measure/initiative; for example, as was the case with the '*Easy*' leaflets posted in those areas of Durham experiencing high numbers of thefts from insecure vehicles.

Box 7.3: REACT

Reassurance: tell the potential victims that they are not being personally 'singled out' but that it is because they are part of a wider demographic or social grouping (for example, they live in a 'hot-spot area', or they live alone).

Empower: frame the proposed crime prevention initiative as a way of empowering people to better protect themselves, their families, and their possessions by improving their security behaviour.

Ask: a sample of the potential victims whether the crime prevention initiative makes sense to them, before deciding to go ahead with it.

Carefully explain: if/when asked by the potential victims, why this kind of intervention is being used (for example, there have been a lot of cars stolen that were left unlocked overnight in this area).

Tell: the potential victims the results of the crime prevention initiative (that is, whether it worked or not and why).

The point here is not to dodge the victim blaming issue by spinning crime prevention messages to the point whereby those identified as being 'high potential victims' are spared from being made aware that they are – this is totally counterproductive – but for police (and other crime prevention agencies) to work at fostering a feeling of empowerment with them. That is, that potential victims should feel that they have some control about whether they become victims or not. The old saying that 'you can lead a horse to water, but you cannot make it drink' may ring true if they forget or decide not to go along with a crime prevention initiative, but they should not be blamed for not drinking any more than police should be blamed for leading them to the water. End of annoying analogies (for now).

Chapter summary

Presented in this chapter was how psychology can and should be used by police and others to inform the prevention of crime, along with an exploration of what can be done using several crime prevention approaches; namely, Clarke's Situational Crime Prevention (1997) and Thaler and Sunstein's *Nudge* (2008). Examples include the adoption of a nudge approach to reducing thefts from insecure vehicles and guidance on how to devise nudges is presented (NUDGE-IT). Finally, suggestions are made for how to counter accusations that giving prevention advice to potential victims is tantamount to blaming them for being victims of crime, with the REACT acronym presented.

Further reading

Clarke, R.V.G. (ed) (1997) *Situational Crime Prevention: Successful Studies* (2nd edn), Albany, NY: Harrow and Heston.

Pease, K., Ignatans, D., and Batty, L. (2018) 'Whatever happened to repeat victimisation?', *Crime Prevention and Community Safety*, 20: 256–67.

Roach, J., Weir, K., Phillips, P., Gaskell, K., and Walton, M. (2016) 'Nudging down theft from insecure vehicles: a pilot study', *International Journal of Police Science and Management*, 19(1): 31–8.

Thaler, R. and Sunstein, C.R. (2008) *Nudge: Improving Decisions about Health, Wealth, and Happiness*, London: Penguin.

Wortley, R., Sidebottom, A., Tilley, N., and Laycock, G. (eds) (2019) *Routledge Handbook of Crime Science*, Abingdon: Routledge.

Suggested resources

https://popcenter.asu.edu/

https://whatworks.college.police.uk/Pages/default.aspx

http://www.telegraph.co.uk/news/2016/06/10/michael-goves-guide-to-britains-greatest-enemy-the-experts/ (accessed 2 September 2016).

See Roach (2017) for a listing of the 12 offence categories mimicking those used by the UK National Crime Agency.

8

Psychology and police wellbeing

Introduction

One of the most obvious spaces where psychology and policing interact is the issue of maintaining police and police staff wellbeing.[1] Attending dangerous and/or emotionally charged situations, for example, is often part and parcel of policing, with many police exposed to ever-changing cocktails of risky and potentially traumatic events, on a daily basis. Put simply, 'it comes with the job'. This raises two primary questions for this chapter:

1. how can knowledge gleaned from psychological research help us to identify the common pressures and stressors on the wellbeing of those working in policing (for example, emotional, psychological, and physical effects); and
2. how can this be best translated into appropriate support to help those working in policing maintain a good level of personal wellbeing?

What appears unfathomable, at least until relatively recently, has been the lack of academic research on police wellbeing, despite the unequivocal acceptance that policing is (1) often a dangerous, risky, challenging, and difficult arena within which to work, and therefore (2) those who do so are exposed to potentially traumatic and emotionally charged events on a daily basis. Despite the formal creation of police services in the UK some 200 years ago, it is only in the last few years that police wellbeing has become a popular focus for academic research. Indeed, research in this area is still at best considered to be 'emergent'. In terms of information and wellbeing support guidance and support available to UK police and police staff, the Oscar Kilo (OK) website developed and maintained by the National Police Wellbeing Service is a shining beacon.[2]

To date, most of the research literature pertaining to the effects on police staff has tended to focus on 'front-line' policing (that is, more on 'mainstream policing functions', such as street patrols), perhaps failing to recognise that modern policing is an occupation comprising thousands of different roles, situations, contexts, and responsibilities (Cartwright and Roach, 2021b). As a defence, as with anything else, the research had to start somewhere, and until recently it could be argued that consequently the wellbeing challenges and needs of police and police staff involved in very different policing roles and functions has been overlooked at the expense of a generalisation on 'policing' as a homogenous phenomenon. Road traffic police and counter-terrorism police personnel, for example, will likely be exposed to different potentially traumatic situations and contexts, which suggests that the impact on their personal wellbeing is likely to be very different, as will the support they need to deal with this will be different to those working as call-handlers or crime prevention officers. The emergence of research looking at the effects of specific tasks and roles in policing indicates a shift in thinking that there are no 'one-size-fits-all' solutions to improving and maintaining the wellbeing of those involved with policing (Roach et al, 2018).

This chapter begins with a short presentation of recent research exploring the general impact that working in policing can have on those that do it, before providing an example of how research has begun to explore how working in criminal investigations can have a negative effect on the wellbeing of police investigators, particularly those working in homicide investigations, and how the identification of different coping strategies can be included in training courses and future support interventions for them.

Policing: it's just not good for one's mental health

Although the public might often find police work glamorous and exciting, best exemplified by the endless production of crime- and policing-related novels, films, television series, and 'box sets' served up to feed viewers' seemingly insatiable appetite for crime drama, evidence indicates that those who do the roles portrayed (that is, police) seldom find it so (Huey & Broll, 2015). In fact, as police are more exposed to acute and chronic life stressors at work, it follows that they are therefore at greater risk, consequently, of developing symptoms of poor mental health including stress, anxiety, depression, and post-traumatic stress disorder (PTSD), compared with those in other professions (for example, see Anshel, 2000; Kohan & O'Connor, 2002; Violanti, 2005). A brief description of *stress* and *psychological trauma* now follows.

Stress

Lazarus and Folkman define stress as: 'A particular relationship between the person and the environment that is appraised by the person as taxing or exceeding his or her resources and endangering his or her wellbeing' (1984, p 19). Research has shown that a higher prevalence of stress-related problems is found among police officers than in the public. This can result in such detrimental health effects such as heart disease, cancer, alcohol dependency, drug abuse, and divorce (for example, Anshel, 2000; Kohan & O'Connor, 2002; Violanti, 2005). As stated previously, those working in policing do so in a plethora of circumstances, environments, and contexts, that differ in the levels of stress that they can generate and so increase the risk of 'burnout' (Hawkins, 2001; Kurtz, 2008; Taris et al, 2010; Padyab, Backteman-Erlanson, & Brulin, 2016).

Much of the existing literature identifying negative effects on police wellbeing can be categorised as being either due to the impact of organisational stressors – for example, bureaucracy and its effect on wellbeing (Violanti et al, 2017) – or to the impact of different operational stressors linked with various roles and functions within policing. Operational stressors commonly refer to the nature of the police work; for example, being exposed to traumatic events such as road traffic accidents (RTAs) or being called to incidents of domestic violence (DV). Such stressors can negatively affect officers' wellbeing with, in the most severe of cases, continuous exposure to traumatic events resulting in those individuals' experiencing depression or PTSD (for example, see Greenberg, Brooks, & Dunn, 2015).

Moreover, four different categories of 'police stressors' have been identified: (1) those extrinsic to the organisation, (2) occupational (that is, task/job related), (3) personal, and (4) organisational (for example, Hart et al, 1993; Finn & Tomz, 1996; Abdollahi, 2002). Much of this research has, however, focused on frontline (uniformed) police, such as the effects of dealing with calls for service and patrolling, or on organisational factors including staffing levels (Fyhn et al, 2016).

Psychological trauma

Duckworth defines psychological trauma as: 'Severe emotional and mental disruption which can follow the experience of certain kinds of extreme events – including those where there is no physical injury' (1991, p 35). Experiencing trauma and the psychological effects, which might follow as a direct consequence, has received much research attention (for example, see Maceachern et al, 2011). One of the most attended to, PTSD, is presented in Box 8.1.

Box 8.1: Post-traumatic stress disorder (PTSD)

PTSD is defined by the *International Classification of Diseases* 11th edition as a disorder which occurs after:

> exposure to an extremely threatening or horrific event or series of events that is characterized by all the following:
>
> 1. re-experiencing the traumatic event or events in the present in the form of vivid intrusive memories, flashbacks, or nightmares, which are typically

accompanied by strong and overwhelming emotions such as fear or horror and strong physical sensations, or feelings of being overwhelmed or immersed in the same intense emotions that were experienced during the traumatic event;

2. avoidance of thoughts and memories of the event or events, or avoidance of activities, situations, or people reminiscent of the event or events; and
3. persistent perceptions of heightened current threat, for example as indicated by hypervigilance or an enhanced startle reaction to stimuli such as unexpected noises. (ICD-11, 2018)[3]

Source: Cartwright and Roach, 2021a

For PTSD to be diagnosed, the symptoms (shown in Box 8.1) must (1) be considered to have endured for a minimum of two weeks and (2) be seen to have substantially impaired a person's life (for example, they have been unable to sleep or to concentrate). It is often more straightforward to diagnose PTSD for those who have experienced an identifiable traumatic incident 'first-hand' (for example, they were either present during an earthquake or an act of terrorism). What is less clear-cut is when people present symptoms associated with PTSD who have not been exposed 'directly' to an identifiable traumatic event, but have experienced one 'second-hand', vicariously through those that have. Police investigators of serious crimes often witness the aftermath of extreme violence, so will often be exposed to the danger of 'vicarious trauma'; it is therefore commonplace for them to experience and empathise trauma to others – for example, attending the scene of a violent crime or when interviewing bereaved relatives of homicide victims (Roach et al, 2018).

Although some police personnel will unfortunately meet the full diagnostic criteria for PTSD, as they have actually witnessed a traumatic event directly (for example, where a colleague was shot in front of them by a suspect resisting arrest or was violently attacked by a member of the public), it is more common for more to experience the effects of secondary trauma; for example, when having to inform parents of the death of their missing child. When an individual experiences negative effects on their wellbeing 'indirectly', it is referred to in different (albeit synonymous) terms, including *secondary traumatic stress* (STS) (Figley, 1995), *compassion fatigue* (Figley, 2002), and *vicarious trauma* (McCann & Pearlman, 1990). The concept of secondary trauma has been widely studied over the last 30 years and is universally considered as exposure to trauma through the first-hand account or narrative of a traumatic event by another (see, for example, Figley, 1995; Foley, Hassett, and Williams, 2021). It has been described as an occupational hazard of working in a caring profession (for example, McCann and Pearlman, 1990), which unfortunately does pose the danger of playing down both its importance and prevalence.

A few years ago, I interviewed several police officers that were working on the night of the terror attack at the Manchester Arena, in 2017. All reported that the most distressing part of the investigation was informing parents that their children had been murdered, rather than witnessing the distressing aftermath of the attack itself. STS is therefore likely to pose a significant threat to the wellbeing of those involved with serious, and emotionally charged, crimes, but should not be seen as 'routine' or simply 'part of the job'.

To revisit a central pillar of this chapter, although, albeit unintentionally (and probably as a result of having to start research in this area somewhere) the common perception might be that all police and police staff face the same potential trauma hazards and so all are equally exposed to similar potential negative effects on their wellbeing, again this should be considered a gross overgeneralisation. This is, of course, not the reality as (1) policing involves a plethora of different duties, roles, functions, and responsibilities undertaken by those involved in policing (Violanti et al, 2017; Foley & Massey, 2019), and (2) not all potentially traumatic events will traumatise those who experience them, but if so, then not necessarily in the same way. By its nature, policing carries an inherent amount of unpredictability in terms of what any officer may experience during working on any day, week, month, or year. The point here is that negative effects on the wellbeing of police and police staff will depend not just on what they do and what they have been exposed to, but also on who they are as a person. One additional consideration which is impossible to separate is the extent to which an individual's job contributes to their poor mental, emotional, and physical wellbeing (for example, being a police officer) from other 'non-job-related' factors, such as a relationship breakdown, bereavement, or poor mental health generally. A potential chicken-and-egg scenario arises in that 'the job' and 'life outside the job' are interconnected with one affecting the other. Nobody can leave their troubles at home. The chances are though, of course, that the more you are exposed to potentially traumatic events and situations, the more likely you are to be traumatised. It is not a wild leap to assume therefore that those who routinely see the worst of human behaviour, such as violent crime, will be more susceptible consequently to negative assaults on their wellbeing (Roach et al, 2016, 2018; Cartwright and Roach, 2021a).

Let us now briefly explore some of the research conducted to identify the negative effects that investigations of serious crimes can have on those police and police staff involved.

Watching the detectives (wellbeing)

Although research to date has explored how some police duties often produce 'work-related stress', such as attending RTAs and exposure to critical incidents involving a death (for example, see He et al, 2002; Liberman et al,

2002), little has focused on the different types and levels of work-related stress experienced by criminal investigators and, more specifically, those investigating homicide.[4] Salo and Allwood suggest that although officers on patrol have stressful events imposed on them from the outside and in real time (for example, breaking up a fight at a bar), stress experienced by criminal investigators 'may still be very real'; for example, when meeting the families of murder victims (2011, p 98).

If we consider the common operational duties of homicide investigators, then it is safe to state that the danger of exposure to both primary trauma (for example, being continually exposed to the death of a human being) and secondary trauma, which occurs through indirect exposure (for example, hearing accounts from witnesses and family and friends about the death of a loved one), is likely to be different and more acute than for those working in other areas of policing (for example, policing crowds or working on burglary investigations). It is important to restate that it is not only the case that exposure to primary traumatic events can produce severe mental distress and a deterioration in officers' wellbeing, but also that exposure to secondary traumatic events can also result in traumatic symptoms, posing a real danger for homicide investigators (Figley, 1995; Newell & MacNeil, 2010; Roach et al, 2017, 2018).

Identifying variations in types and levels of stress experienced by police investigators of different types of crime has received little attention to date. In a study by Fyhn et al (2016) of how different investigators dealt with different types of victim trauma, Norwegian police investigators were assigned to one of two groups: those who investigated 'assault crime' and those who investigated 'fire, forensics, financial, and environmental' crime. The prime focus of the study was 'hardiness', a personality style previously found to influence an individual's ability to cope with stressors in constructive ways comprising three factors: challenge, control, and commitment (Kobasa, Maddi, & Kahn, 1982). Interestingly, 'commitment' was found to be significantly higher in participants who investigated assault crimes, than in the fire, forensics, financial, and environmental crime investigator group (Fyhn et al, 2016). The assault crime investigator group also reported significantly higher levels of social support available to them, higher levels of meaningfulness regarding how they perceived the work that they do, and higher levels of subjective health problems, than their counterparts in the other investigator group (Fyhn et al, 2016). 'Social support' (for example, work colleagues and family) in the work environment and 'hardiness commitment' were found to be particularly important in explaining resilience to stress self-reported by the 'assault crime' investigator group (Fyhn et al, 2016). Now enter the stereotypical battle-hardened, can handle anything, murder detective then?

That said, despite the serious and disturbing acts of criminality which are investigated by police and police staff, few studies have explored the different ways and intensity that investigating serious crimes, such as murder, can have psychologically and emotionally on those who investigate them. Again, this is somewhat surprising considering what the research tells us about trauma causation and the logic that being involved with such serious investigations, often comprising extreme violence and harm, increases the risks of psychological trauma for those involved (Roach et al, 2016, 2018).

So, what does the current research tell us about the effects of serious crime investigation on police investigators, how do they deal with those effects (that is, cope), and how can research be translated into practical help and support for maintaining their wellbeing and mental health? The next section summarises the literature to date in terms of what we know. We start with the general effects on the wellbeing of police investigators before moving on to those identified with those involved with specific investigation types and roles.

General negative effects on the wellbeing of police investigators

The results of a study involving 601 serving UK police officers, conducted by Brown et al (1999), provides a useful breakdown of roles typically required by criminal investigators along with the levels of stress reported (that is, average stress score reported) and is presented in Table 8.1.

As can be seen in Table 8.1, the police participants reported that different roles and functions they experienced within a criminal investigation tended to produce varying levels of stress, with those associated with investigating

Table 8.1: Stress levels of roles required within criminal investigation

Dealing with/responding to	Mean stress level
Cot death	3.28
Sudden death	3.17
Sex abuse victim	2.98
Sudden death message	2.68
Suicide	2.37
Rape statement	2.33
Initial rape complaint	2.27
Sex offence victim	2.06
Domestic violence victims	1.76
Violence victims	1.62
Missing child	1.62
Missing adult	1.14

Source: Brown et al, 1999

crimes committed against the most vulnerable reported as being most stressful (Brown et al, 1999).

Investigating homicide

Van Patten and Burke used a variety of different psychological tests to identify cognitive functioning, psychological effects, and levels of psychopathology, in a sample of 67 US police investigators, all who were experienced in the investigation of adult and child homicide (Van Patten & Burke, 2001). Their findings suggest that although those involved with child homicide investigations experienced much higher levels of stress-related symptoms than would be found in the general 'non-police' population, these were not higher than scores found for psychiatric outpatients (Van Patten & Burke, 2001).

Although the Van Pattern and Burke (2001) findings are interesting, as they suggest that the investigation of a suspicious child death is likely to have a larger negative effect on the psychological and emotional wellbeing of those doing the investigating, this is inconclusive for two main reasons: (1) it is difficult to determine whether such effects were a direct result of investigating these cases, or whether it was in fact more a general cumulative consequence of their involvement in a large number of homicide investigations per se, and (2) it is likely that this sample of investigators would have investigated significantly more adult victim homicides than child victims, simply because adult victim homicides are much more prevalent (Roach and Bryant, 2015; Roach et al, 2018).

Further exploration of the different detrimental effects on the wellbeing of those involved in adult and child victim homicide investigations has been conducted by Roach and colleagues (Roach, Cartwright, and Sharratt, 2016; 2018). In a study including 99 UK police homicide investigators, the findings suggest the existence of different and more acute effects on investigator wellbeing in cases of child homicide. Employing an online survey to explore whether (and if so how) potentially negative effects on homicide investigator wellbeing differed according to whether the victims were adults or children, 99 experienced UK homicide investigators reported investigating child homicides as having 'greater negative effects' on their personal wellbeing. Differences reported included experiencing higher levels of intrusive thoughts, more negative emotional reactions, higher perceived levels of investigative complexity, and more pressure to resolve the case satisfactorily (Roach et al, 2016).

In the same study, it was also found that that investigators who reported not having been involved with a child homicide investigation for at least six months prior to the study stated that these investigations had most detrimentally affected their wellbeing when compared with investigators who had not had an interval of up to six months since their last child homicide investigation, or who had not had a gap in time at all (Roach et al, 2016). We explain this finding by suggesting it likely that those more regularly involved with child homicide investigations may not have the luxury of the 'headspace' necessary with which to process and begin to address the possible negative effects that these investigations have had on their wellbeing. In terms of supporting those involved with child homicide investigations, the findings of this study strongly suggest that the danger for regular investigators of child homicide is in fact the build-up of 'negative cumulative effects' on their wellbeing, which might eventually lead to acute and profound trauma effects, when unacknowledged (Roach et al, 2016). Moreover, and rather worryingly, that 'investigator experience' did not appear to help mitigate the emotional assaults on investigator wellbeing in child homicides, with the most experienced and less experienced appearing to be equally susceptible to negative impacts on their personal wellbeing (Roach et al, 2016).

In a further study employing semi-structured interviews with UK and Danish police homicide investigators, myself and colleagues (Roach, Sharratt, Cartwright, and Skou Roer, 2018) found that homicide investigations involving child victims of extreme violence, where the victim was of a similar age to the investigators' own children, impacted most negatively on investigator wellbeing. All of their homicide investigator participants identified the death of a child, particularly a young child, to be significantly more complex in terms of the investigation processes involved (for example, coroners' verdicts establishing cause of death) than with adult victim homicide investigations, and often thereby more likely to have an effect on their wellbeing for longer than in adult homicide investigations (Roach et al, 2018).

In a study of 56 Slovenian homicides, sexual offences, and juvenile crimes, criminal investigator participants were asked to complete numerous psychometric questionnaires to identify any coping strategies that they employed, alongside levels of self-reported psychological ill-health (for example, regarding post-traumatic stress symptomology – see Pavšič Mrevlje, 2016). 7.4 per cent of the investigator sample reported experiencing 'clinically significant' symptoms of PTSD, with a further 3.7 per cent reporting experiencing 'milder' PTSD symptoms. Interestingly, although five participants who reported high levels of post-traumatic stress symptoms worked in the 'juvenile crime' area of policing, only one homicide and sexual offences investigator reported having high levels of PTSD symptomology. Additionally, it was found that investigators tended to employ more 'avoidance coping strategies', which raises obvious concerns for their wellbeing, as avoidance coping strategies generally result in poor long-term wellbeing outcomes (Pavšič Mrevlje, 2016).

Investigating sexual offences

Another area of criminal investigative work identified as high risk in terms of its potential risk to investigator wellbeing is sexual offence cases. For example, in a study examining levels of STS with civilian police specialist investigators working in violent and sexual offending teams, psychometric testing found evidence of mild STS among these specialist investigators (Gray & Rydon-Grange, 2019). The same study reported no differences with regards the gender of the 'special investigators', and that 'length of service' was only related to increased levels of STS for 'very new investigators' (see Cartwright and Roach, 2021a) suggesting on the whole that experienced investigators were equally susceptible to STS symptomology, echoing the findings of the Roach et al (2016) study of UK homicide investigators. Perhaps most importantly, the authors reported that those special investigators identified as having 'insecure and avoidant attachment styles', were found to be at higher risk of STS, whereas those scoring higher on 'mindfulness and coping self-efficacy' were found to be at decreased risk (Gray & Rydon-Grange, 2019). This suggests that personality and other individual differences are important considerations when supporting and maintaining investigator wellbeing (Cartwright and Roach, 2021a).

Parkes, Graham-Kevan, & Bryce (2019) in a study of wellbeing effects reported that sexual offence investigations often had a negative effect on investigator wellbeing; for example, by intruding into their personal lives, producing symptoms of PTSD, and influencing changes in their personal view of the world.

Investigating child abuse and child sexual exploitation

Modern advances in mass communication, such as the internet and social media, provide opportunities to facilitate old types of crime (for example, child grooming) and the creation of new ones, such as 'trolling' (Cartwright and Roach, 2021a). One of the worst ways in which these have facilitated criminality is arguably the ease with which videos and photos of children being sexually abused can be made, accessed, shared, and distributed on a scale incomparable prior to their invention.

As part of the investigation, and then the criminal prosecution process, police investigators are required to analyse and examine what is abhorrent and emotionally damaging video evidence, for both victim and perpetrator identification and evidential purposes (Akdeniz, 2008). It does not take a great leap of the imagination to assume that frequent exposure to such traumatic and disturbing imagery is likely to have a negative effect on the wellbeing of those involved with these types of investigation.

Burns et al (2008) studied the wellbeing effects with a sample of Canadian online child sexual exploitation (CSE) investigators, and identified 'affect symptoms' including intrusive thoughts, headaches, irritable mood, and extreme fatigue, all of which are consistent with symptoms related to STS. This study also found a number of coping and support methods used by the CSE investigators including the *viewing strategy* they used, *access to psychological support*, *availability of peer* and *social support*, *use of humour*, and *initial candidate selection* (that is, they were better suited to the role than others) (Burns et al, 2008). The Burns et al (2008) study also outlined a number of categories hindered their coping, including: the *criminal justice system* (for example, its slowness), *amount of time spent viewing the evidence*, a *lack of investigative resources*, *various psychological interventions*, and *organisational factors*, which included high workloads.

Similarly, in a study by Stevenson (2007) with participants comprising supervisors of online child sexual abuse investigations, involvement with this type of investigative work was reported to cause emotional distress, with greater extent and intensity of exposure to such disturbing images resulting in a higher severity of the emotional distress reported (Stevenson, 2007). Furthermore, it was reported that the supervisors demonstrated a number of additional wellbeing issues, including, worries regarding inappropriate sexual thoughts and exhaustion (Stevenson, 2007).

Research by Perez et al (2010) used self-report data relating to burnout and STS by psychometric measures with a US sample of online CSE investigators and found that 18 per cent of their sample of investigators showed *high levels of STS*, with a further 18 per cent showing *moderate levels of STS*. On a more positive note, *social support* was found to help reduce the risk of STS and burnout.

Bourke and Craun (2014) explored levels of STS in 288 UK and 677 US online child abuse investigators. They found that UK investigators reported significantly lower levels of STS when compared with their US counterparts. Furthermore, it was reported that in the US participants, 15 per cent of investigators reported symptoms associated with severe STS, whereas this was reported in only 10 per cent of UK participants. Bourke and Craun (2014) identified 'predictors' of high levels of symptoms as an increased exposure to indecent child images and with higher self-reported levels of difficulty of working with the material. This was the same for both UK and US investigators, with reporting of increased alcohol and tobacco usage in the past year and the denial of any stress occurring as a result of the investigative work (Bourke and Craun, 2014). Looking at potential mitigating factors in terms of high STS, again being able to rely on the support of co-workers was found to significantly reduce levels of STS. In a further study by Craun et al (2015) with a large sample of US investigators of online crimes against children, only 27 per cent of investigators stated that their work had no effect on their family life, with the majority reporting changes, such as: distrusting others more (24 per cent), withdrawing from family and friends (14 per cent), improvement in their relationships (10 per cent), inability to talk to others about their work (9.4 per cent), alongside other more infrequently reported changes (Craun et al 2015).

Similar findings have also been reported by Tehrani (2016) who conducted a study with 126 UK internet child abuse investigators. Although Tehrani's research specifically examined STS and burnout in investigators, it also measured symptoms of anxiety and depression and found that 16 per cent of male and 24 per cent of female investigators had demonstrated cut-off scores suggestive of early PTSD; 24 per cent of male and 38 per cent of female investigators demonstrated early symptoms of burnout; 16 per cent of male and 38 per cent of female investigators displayed early symptoms of anxiety; 12 per cent of male and 26 per cent of female investigators demonstrated early symptoms of depression; and finally 16 per cent of male and 22 per cent of female investigators reported scores indicative of early symptoms of STS. Finally, MacEachern et al (2018) reported that 11 per cent of their sample had STS symptoms in the high to severe range, with 51 per cent seeming to experience some degree of STS symptomology. Although no significant differences in STS scores between males and females were found, it was only female participants that met the threshold for high to severe STS.

We finish with the effects on wellbeing as a result of doing the job, as experienced by some of those involved in criminal investigations who often really do see the worst side of human behaviour – crime scene investigators.

Crime scene investigation

In the UK, scenes of crime officers (SOCOs) tend to be civilian police staff who routinely examine scenes of crimes to collect forensic evidence, including crimes of violence and/or abuse and neglect. Yet again, the possible negative effects on wellbeing of this group is at best under-researched and at worst neglected, with very few published studies to date exploring the psychological and wellbeing effects of those in this role (Sollie et al, 2017). That said, what research has been produced to date is briefly presented next.

Yoo et al (2013), in a study with 111 Korean crime scene investigators, found that 42.3 per cent were reported attending homicide scenes 1–2 times per week, 45.1 per cent 3–4 times per week, and 12.6 per cent more than 5 times per week. Most significantly, those who had investigated homicides 3–4 times per week displayed significantly higher post-traumatic stress symptom scores than other investigators (Yoo et al, 2013). Furthermore, the researchers found that: *less experience* as a crime scene investigator, *higher levels of death anxiety*, a *type A personality*, and *lower emotional intelligence* were all associated with higher PTSD symptom scores (Yoo et al, 2013). Despite the identification of risk factors that increased PTSD scores, these researchers found that levels of PTSD symptoms were lower than was previously found in research with firefighters; however, no comparison with the general population was made. Similarly, in a more recent study based on a sample of 226 Korean crime scene investigators, Nho and Kim (2017) reported that 19.9 per cent were found to be in the high-risk group for PTSD. *Social support and resilience* were found to be factors associated with the low-risk group, leading the authors to suggest that wellbeing intervention programmes and training should focus upon developing these (Nho & Kim, 2017). How do these findings manifest in terms of staff happiness and retention?

A study of crime scene investigators in Australia found attrition rates of up to 50 per cent for crime scene investigator posts; however, surprisingly depression and anxiety levels measured were lower than that found for the general population. suggesting, at face-value at least, few negative effects on their wellbeing as an actual result of 'doing the job' (Kelty & Gordon, 2015).

Sollie et al (2017) focused on stress induced by crime scene investigating in the Netherlands, as opposed to specifically measuring trauma, identified 'deployment stressors' such as workload, 'disturbed sleep patterns', 'irregular work patterns', and 'administrative procedures' along with several stressors were found to be associated with the 'impact of the crime scene investigation work'. Investigators outlined a number of emotional triggers associated with their work including: '(a) the type of victim, (b) the way in which the crime was committed, (c) identifying with the victim, (d) the circumstances of death, and (e) contact with bereaved relatives' (Sollie et al, 2017, p 1589). In the same study, crime scene investigators reported a number of 'coping styles and techniques' which they believed had allowed them to continue their work, some being positive and some negative, including: *avoidance* (whereby they opt not to attend a particular crime scene that may cause emotional distress), *emotionally distancing themselves* (that is, seeing victims as evidence and not human beings), *seeking social support*, and *visualisation* (whereby they prepare themselves through visualising the crime scene prior to visiting) (Sollie et al, 2017).

Chapter summary

This chapter has explored how psychological research and policing can interact when examining how police work can negatively affect the wellbeing of police personnel. The brief review of the research in this area presented here suffices to demonstrate the existence of different types and levels of impact on police wellbeing, according to different types of police work, including different types of criminal investigation: *general investigative work*, *child sexual abuse investigation*, and *crime scene investigation*.

Research has identified a number of different factors that impact negatively on police investigator wellbeing, primarily those investigations where the victim was a vulnerable individual (particularly a young child). In terms of coping with negative wellbeing effects, common factors identified by all studies to date are the importance of *social support*, with those reporting as having poor social support being at greater risk of experiencing negative wellbeing effects, and those with good social support seemingly at less risk. This suggests that future wellbeing and training interventions for professionals involved in criminal investigation work should focus on building up investigators' resilience to cope in this area.

One of the current limitations of research in this area is the paucity of wellbeing studies which use standardised psychometric tools to measure negative effects on investigator wellbeing, although there is evidence that this about to change (Cartwright and Roach, 2021a). At the moment though, this makes it difficult to compare the levels of wellbeing and psychopathology across different police roles and between national and international forces. Therefore, future research is required using standardised psychological instruments such as the STS Disorder scale (Bride et al, 2004). This is particularly encouraged as it should help us to achieve a more comprehensive understanding of individual risk of police personnel developing severe negative traumatic responses to working in criminal investigations, facilitating the development of more effective, and more tailored, support services.

This chapter concludes with an echo of Cartwright and Roach's (2021a) original plea for researchers in this area to consider three key questions associated with maintaining criminal investigator wellbeing:

1. What are the effects and how do we recognise them?
2. How and when they are most likely to influence and manifest (for example, different investigator roles and functions)?
3. How can we help our criminal investigators be better prepared, protected, and safeguarded against these potential assaults on their wellbeing?

In terms of resources for police and police staff to draw upon, the reader is again directed to the excellent Oscar Kilo website.[5]

Further reading

Foley, J. and Massey, K. (2019) 'Police officers and post-traumatic stress disorder: discussing the deficit in research, identification and prevention in England and Wales', *The Police Journal: Theory, Practice and Principles*, 92(1): 23–34.

Roach, J., Cartwright, A., and Sharratt, K. (2016). 'Dealing with the unthinkable: a study of the cognitive and emotional stress of adult and child homicide investigations on police investigators', *Journal of Police and Criminal Psychology*, 32(3): 251–62.

Violanti, J., Charles, L., McCanlies, E. et al (2017) 'Police stressors and health: a state-of-the art review', *Policing*, 40(4): 642–56.

For a collection of research papers exploring police wellbeing, the reader is directed to the recent 'Are we Okay' special edition of *The Police Journal: Theory, Practice and Principles*, 95(1). Available at: https://journals.sagepub.com/toc/pjxa/95/1

Suggested resources

For all things relating to UK police wellbeing, visit https://oscarkilo.org.uk/national-police-wellbeing-service/

9

Psychology and policing: taking stock and where do we go from here?

Introduction

If, like me, you have never seen the point of the last chapter of a book merely summarising (that is, basically repeating) the chapters that have gone before, then rest assured that it is not happening here. This chapter is therefore short, to encourage the reader to get the impression that this book is more of a beginning than an end, more of a work in progress than fait accompli. If achieved, then it is hoped it will ether provoke or stimulate further thought as to where the relationship between psychological research and knowledge and policing might need to focus and develop in the future.

Hopefully, having now convinced the reader of the valuable contribution that psychology has and can make in the future – for example, regarding advancements in the interviewing of suspects and witnesses, the enhancing of investigative decision-making, and with the prevention of crime – how the relationship between both might be advanced is the obvious next question. I am not so conceited as to think that I alone possess a metaphorical roadmap for how any relationship needs to go, I merely intend to make some suggestions for likely areas where it might wish to stop off on the journey.

'The dating game': in search of the ideal relationship between police and academic researchers

The only advice that I ever give when anybody asks me about their 'relationships' or for that matter any 'affairs of the heart' is, first, not to ask for any such advice in the first place, and second, not to offer any advice about such matters under any circumstances. Unless that is you are particularly adept at negotiating your way through 'emotional minefields'. In my experience at least, that way disaster lies, particularly in the shape of an angry friend with whom you agreed that indeed their relationship was over, but which turns out several months later, not to be the case.

Any advice given here is solely meant to foster and forge productive relationships between police and academics, so that the chances of me being held responsible for any emotional car crash that might ensue are minimal enough to make it a rare exception. The more difficult question is how to achieve a meaningful, productive, and mutually beneficial relationship between police and academic researchers, and to this end I humbly offer my six top tips for a forging a good (and sustainable) police and researcher relationship.

A relationship between police and academia must be one of equal partnership

This is crucial if the relationship is to stand any hope of reducing the particular crime and policing-related problem for which the relationship has come together in the first place. Although some may cringe when I say this, I truly believe that research must be something done 'with police' and not 'to them'.

A relationship must be one of mutual benefit

Apparently, any stable and lasting relationship is built on solid foundations. Academic researchers courting police collaboration are therefore advised to make it clear from the very start just how their research is likely to be of benefit to police. This can of course take many forms; for example, by helping sharpen a particular police practice by evidence-based research, or perhaps by informing how police thinking might be changed or enhanced by promoting a greater awareness of patterns of offending, such as with Ken Pease and my work on *Self-Selection Policing*. Still (sadly) too much criminological research is missed or ignored because it is badly packaged, promising little practical utility for police officers or indeed to anyone else. Put bluntly, if a second date is to happen, then areas of likely mutual benefit must be identified early so as to prevent any damaging misunderstandings and disappointments later on.

Find common ground and use a common language

I once read in a magazine that 'a secure relationship is based on good communication'. A good police and academic relationship needs to be one where both sides understand what their roles are, what parts they play, and what is being actually asked and expected of them. That way mutual and informed consent lies. Without a commonly understood language then any researcher–police relationship will be akin to a 'my wife doesn't understand me' scenario and will most likely end in tears. For example, academic researchers should not obsess about p-values without explaining, if need be, what they are and why they are important. Suffice to say here that p-value (probability value) tells us how likely it is that our data could have occurred under the null hypothesis. But you see my point!

Establish mutual trust

Some academic researchers pay lip service to confidentiality and sell their souls in a Faustian pact with the media without thought for the feelings and sensibilities of police officers, crime victims, and their families. Mercifully, these are few in number and do not work with police for long. Although a brief relationship might get them a book deal to produce a publication of the nature found in airport travel shops, a second date is unlikely and they go home alone, probably in an expensive taxi.

Remember academic researchers and police are not mutually exclusive

Police officers are often best placed to identify need and carry out relevant research, particularly with appropriate support and encouragement from academics. The reporting of useful research does not only have to be in academic journals (as most are impossible for police to access) whereby publication in professional magazines is often a much better way of reaching 'people on the ground'. This holds for academic-based research, whereby academic researchers are encouraged to not just publish in academic-focused journals but to also write in plain English in publications that time-strapped police read. A common term used in the UK for those who ride both academic and police practitioner horses is 'pracademic'. I'm not sure I like the term as in my mind it doesn't matter which you consider yourself to be most, research is research (as long as it is evidence-based of course).

Where possible, academics should have police colleagues working on research projects alongside them

I am fortunate to say that I have many ex-police colleagues that I often work with on research projects, without whom most of my research to date would not have been possible. I recently asked a detective colleague whether he had ever received training on cognitive bias and he answered me with an emphatic 'no', encouraging me to develop a one-day workshop for SIOs focusing on the perils and pitfalls of cognitive bias in criminal investigations. I hope that the fact we decided to co-deliver it added an authenticity with police attendees, and helped smooth over any potential perceptions of 'being talked to by a professor who has never done the job' that any attendees might have anticipated.

Unfortunately, brevity dictates the shortness of my list so please do not consider it a prescription for wedded bliss. It is perhaps more fitting to consider it a template for the basis of a prenuptial agreement.

The end of the beginning?

At a risk of labouring the point, this book was never meant to be an end in itself, but more of an end of the beginning. Of course, there are many other areas of policing which psychological research and theory have, and continue, to touch which have been overlooked in this book, such as psychology and police recruitment or psychology and police training and learning. This is not to say that any omitted areas have been deemed less worthy of inclusion, simply that with this book I have focused on areas which many other psychology and policing books (of which there are still not many) have either not covered or have done so with less of a practical focus. So how and where should future psychological research for policing go?

To address the how, future psychological research will need to continue to be 'naturalistic' as well as 'traditional'. Although breakthroughs in more general psychological research can hold important implications for police and policing – for example, in terms of memory recall, treating trauma, or understanding radicalisation – more research needs to be done with police in their 'natural' policing environments, which is what the focus of this book has tried to demonstrate. Findings from decision-making research, for example, should not simply be imported into a police/policing context from cognitive research conducted with student participants in laboratories, but should be the product of both research with police participants using policing (rather than everyday) scenarios, and from observing how police make decisions in policing situations and environments, particularly where decisions have to be made quickly and in dangerous situations.

An internet of thieves!

One increasingly important area for psychological and practically focused research and knowledge for policing is, of course, the internet, as more and more crime is committed via the World Wide Web. 'Cybercrime' includes both new crimes, only possible because of the invention of the 'Web' (for example, 'phishing', 'trolling', and certain types of 'identity theft') and crimes as 'old wine in new bottles' whereby well-known types of crime, such as benefit fraud, child abuse, and tax evasion, can be facilitated by use of the internet.

Psychological research needs to focus, for example, on how different types of cybercrime can be prevented and policed as traditional means of prevention and policing (for example, criminal investigation) will become increasingly less suited to identifying those committing them, with changes in the investigation of CSE being a recent example.

Indeed, the creation of the World Wide Web is arguably the most shiny example of a complete lack of 'crime thinking' and naivety. Did no one foresee that the internet would be used and exploited for criminal purposes, or did we all really think that it would only be used to do 'nice things', like tracing long, lost relatives or making it easier to book a holiday? Well the cybercrime horse has well and truly bolted, the offender genie has come out of the lamp, and so on and so on as most crime prevention interventions to reduce different types of cybercrime tend to be retrofitted, rather than built-in at the point of being brought to market. Psychology can help policing here or at least future research into offender decision-making in cyberspace will; for example, how to put someone off who is about to steal the online identity of another.

Another area where psychological research might better inform policing practice is in the prevention of crime; for example, how might the 'nudge' approach be developed and better employed and targeted to encourage internet users to think and behave in a more security-conscious way, in terms of protecting their finances and reputations from criminals. For example, the common messaging currently being used to provoke us into taking more care of our data and online identities is similar to the previous messages used to remind us to lock our vehicles, akin to the 'lock it or lose it' mantra. As suggested in Chapter 7, such generic and ill-targeted messaging is unlikely to touch a large percentage of the public, and more likely to simply wash over their heads. As the Durham 'nudge' study (Roach et al, 2016) highlights, crime prevention messaging needs to be more sophisticated and better targeted if it is to stand a better chance of influencing behaviour. Cybersecurity messaging needs to follow the same path.

Ken Pease and I are currently thinking about how SSP thinking might be employed to help identify serious criminality on the internet from minor infractions of the law. We might not be there yet, but suffice to say that we both accept that this is the natural direction for SSP to take. So money where mouths are time!

Police wellbeing

If I had taken even longer to finish writing this book than I actually did (which was far longer than I ever imagined and am quite embarrassed about) then I have no doubt that the chapter on police wellbeing would have reflected the tsunami of research currently in the publication process. As the editor of *The Police Journal: Theory, Practice and Principles*, currently 1 in 5 papers submitted to us concerns empirical study or commentary on police wellbeing. Alas, much of the research is still to be published, but what has begun to be looked into is how different areas of policing and various roles can have a negative effect on police wellbeing; for example, on police homicide investigators (Roach, Cartwright, and Sharratt, 2016; Roach, Sharratt, Cartwright, and Skou Roer, 2018). Hopefully, the contribution that psychology will make in helping to improve the wellbeing of police will continue to grow and make it one of the most important 'service station stops' on the 'relationship road' between practical psychology and policing. The wellbeing of police personnel while working during the pandemic is most likely to be a common thread in the very near future.

Some readers may consider the omission of occupational psychology and its beneficial impact on police wellbeing, a fatal flaw for any book purporting to be about psychology and policing. In my defence, this omission is not because I disagree with the importance of occupational psychology to policing; on the contrary, I believe that it deserves/warrants a dedicated book and I encourage those readers thinking of writing such a book to do so. It is very important. Merely that I had begged enough time to finish the book already. If it makes it to a second edition, then I will include it.

And finally, finally

As this book is not an end (at best the end of a beginning) then please do contact me with any ideas that you might have. As I said right at the beginning of this book, some of the research presented is based upon ideas that I have had, but equally much is based on the ideas of others – particularly those in policing – which I have helped to be born. If you feel the need for an 'ideas midwife', then I guess I'm your man!

Notes

Chapter 1

1 'Minority Report' is a 2002 film by Twentieth Century Fox, directed by Steven Spielberg.
2 Available at https://dictionary.apa.org/tacit-knowledge.
3 And please do contact me if you do!

Chapter 2

1 https://www.oxfordlearnersdictionaries.com/definition/english/science?q=science
2 https://www.ucl.ac.uk/jill-dando-institute/
3 https://popcenter.asu.edu/
4 See https://dictionary.cambridge.org/dictionary/english/craft.
5 https://www.college.police.uk/research/evidence-based-policing-EBP
6 https://whatworks.college.police.uk/About/Pages/What-is-EBP.aspx
7 https://www.crim.cam.ac.uk/research
8 https://www.bps.org.uk/member-microsites/division-forensic-psychology
9 The interested reader is directed to the wonderful work of researchers in this area, such as Jess Woodhams, Craig Bennell, and Gaby Salfati.
10 For example, see Ressler's *Whoever Fights Monsters* (1992), David Canter's *Criminal Shadows* (1994), or Paul Britton's *The Jigsaw Man* (1997).
11 Readers interested in the introduction and development of PACE (1984) are directed to https://www.gov.uk/guidance/police-and-criminal-evidence-act-1984-pace-codes-of-practice.
12 Although further explanation is not provided here, a good account of the PEACE approach can be found at https://www.app.college.police.uk/app-content/investigations/investigative-interviewing/.

Chapter 3

1 'RoboCop' is a 1987 American science fiction action film directed by Paul Verhoeven.
2 https://www.app.college.police.uk/app-content/national-decision-model/
3 As I work on the edits and corrections of the latest draft of this book, Ukraine has just been invaded by Russia.
4 To be fair I did contemplate joining the police a few years ago when I was aged 18. Alas, I thought that for me there appeared two insurmountable obstacles. First, I was not (and am still not) good with hierarchies and police forces depend on them. Second, I didn't at the time fancy swearing an oath/allegiance to the Queen, or anyone else for that matter. I had nothing against her personally, but I did have a thing about monarchies and social inequality, probably attributable to my love for the band The Smiths. None of this will come as any great surprise to anyone who knows me, as clearly, with and without hindsight, I have always been an idiot!
5 Mr D was my magical English teacher to whom I affectionately referred in Chapter 1. If you didn't read Chapter 1, then this reference makes no sense – shame on you!
6 The reader is advised not to purchase a new car when experiencing either extreme happiness or extreme sadness, as emotionality often clouds our decision-making.
7 See https://www.theguardian.com/us-news/2017/jun/26/jobs-future-automation-robots-skills-creative-health for the full article.
8 https://popcenter.asu.edu/content/what-pop
9 See https://popcenter.asu.edu/content/sara-model-1

10 For those readers unfamiliar with the term 'shed' they are usually small, wooden outbuildings commonly found in the gardens of houses where, for example, garden tools, bicycles, and lawnmowers are kept. I fear the shed is probably an English thing as most other people will use a car-garage for such storage purposes. If so, perhaps Napoleon Bonaparte really should have referred to us English as 'a nation of shed-keepers'.

11 Yet another indication that I was delusional at an early age or indeed at any age.

12 For the original version, visit https://www.app.college.police.uk/app-content/national-decision-model/the-national-decision-model/.

13 See https://www.gov.uk/government/publications/sir-lawrence-byford-report-into-the-police-handling-of-the-yorkshire-ripper-case.

14 See https://www.gov.uk/government/publications/sir-lawrence-byford-report-into-the-police-handling-of-the-yorkshire-ripper-case.

Chapter 4

1 See for example http://www.people-records.co.uk/Sex-Offenders-Register.php for more information about the register.

Chapter 5

1 Provided the reader is not a serious criminal, of course. Although I cannot afford to discriminate with my readership!

2 http://www.college.police.uk/Pages/Home.aspx

Chapter 6

1 Sir Robert Peel became Home Secretary in 1822 and in 1829 established the first full-time, professional and centrally organised police force in England and Wales, for the Greater London area. The nine principles that underpin this philosophy were set out in the 'General Instructions' issued to every new police officer from 1829 onwards – see https://thecrimepreventionwebsite.com/police-crime-prevention-service---a-short-history/744/the-peelian-principles/ for further information.

2 Other sprinters are available.

3 http://www.telegraph.co.uk/news/2016/06/10/michael-goves-guide-to-britains-greatest-enemy-the-experts/

4 'Prime Suspect' is a popular British police drama about a female detective, devised by Lynda La Plante and starring Helen Mirren, which ran from 1991 to 2006, produced by Granada Television.

5 'Columbo' is a series about a Los Angeles homicide detective, starring Peter Falk, which ran from 1968 to 1978.

6 See https://en.wikipedia.org/wiki/The_Sweeney or better still watch a few episodes!

7 Top-Down Processing is information processing guided by higher-level mental processes, as when we construct perceptions drawing on our experience and expectations. Perception.

8 These are common feelings that I have, by the way.

9 Again, my career is often like this.

Chapter 7

1 The reader is encouraged to visit the Problem Orientated policing website for all 25 SCP techniques, available at https://popcenter.asu.edu/sites/default/files/twenty_five_techniques_of_situational_prevention.pdf.

2 One reason why many dinosaurs became extinct was that their scaly skins did not adapt (in evolutionary terms) quick enough for them to deal effectively with ice ages.

3 For interesting story, see https://www.newcastleherald.com.au/story/4363061/thieves-attempt-to-steal-atm/.
4 See https://www.bi.team/publications/mindspace/.

Chapter 8

1 I have unashamedly leaned heavily in this chapter on work that I have been fortunate enough to have conducted with my friends and colleagues, Ashly Cartwright, Katherine Sharratt, Thomas Skou Roer, and Liam Curran. I thank you all, but any issues you might have please refer them directly to my lawyer.
2 OK website, available at https://www.oscarkilo.org.uk/.
3 Available at https://icd.who.int/en.
4 For a more detailed review of the research literature relating to police investigator wellbeing, see Cartwright and Roach (2021).
5 https://oscarkilo.org.uk/national-police-wellbeing-service/

References

Abdollahi, M.K. (2002) 'Understanding police stress research', *Journal of Forensic Psychology Practice*, 2(2): 1–24.

Adler, J.R. and Gray, J.M. (eds) (2010) *Forensic Psychology: Concepts, Debates and Practice* (2nd edn), Cullompton: Willan.

Ainsworth, P.B. (2001) *Offender Profiling and Crime Analysis*, Cullompton: Willan.

Ainsworth, P.B. (2002) *Psychology and Policing*, London: Routledge.

Akdeniz, Y. (2008) *Internet Child Pornography and the Law: National and International Responses*, London: Routledge.

Alison, E. and Alison, L. (2020) *Rapport: The Four Ways to Read People*, London: Penguin.

Alison, L. (2005) *The Forensic Psychologist's Casebook: Psychological Profiling and Criminal Investigation*, Cullompton: Willan.

Alison, L., McLean, C., and Almond, L. (2007) 'Profiling suspects', in T. Newburn, T. Williamson, and A. Wright (eds) *Handbook of Criminal Investigation*, Cullompton: Willan, pp 493–516.

Alison, L., Doran, B., Long, M.L., Power, N., and Humphrey, A. (2013) 'The effects of subjective time pressure and individual differences on hypotheses generation and action prioritization in police investigations', *Journal of Experimental Psychology: Applied*, 19(1): 83–93.

Anshel, M. (2000) 'A conceptual model and implications for coping with stressful events in police work', *Criminal Justice Behavior*, 27: 375–400.

Areh, I., Mesko, G., and Umek, P. (2009) 'Attributions of personal characteristics to victims of rape: police officers' perspectives', *Studia Psychologica*, 51: 85–100.

Ashton, J., Brown, I., Senior, B., and Pease, K. (1998) 'Repeat victimisation: offender accounts', *International Journal of Risk, Security and Crime Prevention*, 3(4): 269–79.

Ask, K. and Granhag, P.A. (2007) 'Motivational bias in criminal investigators' judgments of witness reliability', *Journal of Applied Social Psychology*, 37(3): 561–91.

Ask, K. and Landstrom, S. (2010) 'Why emotions matter: expectancy violation and affective response mediate the emotional victim effect', *Law and Human Behavior*, 34(5): 392–401.

Association of Chief Police Officers (ACPO)/Centrex (2005) *Practice Advice on Core Investigative Doctrine*, Bramshill: National Centre for Policing Excellence.

Association of Chief Police Officers of England and Wales (ACPO) (2006) *Murder Investigation Manual*, Bramshill: National Centre for Policing Excellence.

Bellamy, G. (1982) *The Sinner's Congregation*, London: Penguin.

Bennett, T., Holloway, K., and Farrington, D. (2008) 'A review of the effectiveness of Neighbourhood Watch', *Security Journal* 22(2): 143–55.

Bernasco, W. (2008) 'Them again? Same-offender involvement in repeat and near repeat burglaries', *European Journal of Criminology*, 5(4): 411–31.

Blumstein, A., Cohen, J., Roth, J.A., and Visher, C.A. (1986a) *Criminal Careers and 'Career Criminals'*, Vol I, Washington, DC: National Academy Press.

Blumstein, A., Cohen, J., Roth, J.A., and Visher, C.A. (eds) (1986b) *Criminal Careers and 'Career Criminals'*, Vol II, Washington, DC: National Academy Press.

Blumstein, A., Cohen, J., Das, S., and Moitra, S.D. (1988) 'Specialisation and seriousness during adult criminal careers', *Journal of Quantitative Criminology*, 4: 303–45.

Bollingmo, G.C., Wessel, E.O., Eilertsen, D.E., and Magnussen, S. (2008) 'Credibility of the emotional witness: a study of ratings by police investigators', *Psychology, Crime and Law*, 14(1): 29–40.

Bourke, M.L. and Craun, S.W. (2014) 'Secondary traumatic stress among internet crimes against children task force personnel: impact, risk factors, and coping strategies', *Sex Abuse*, 26(6): 586–609.

Bowers, K., Johnson, S., and Pease, K. (2004) 'Prospective hot-spotting: the future of crime mapping?', *British Journal of Criminology*, 44(5): 641–58.

Brantingham, P.J. and Faust, F.L. (1976) 'A conceptual model of crime prevention', *Crime and Delinquency*, 22: 284–96.

Bride B.E., Robinson M.M., Yegidis, B., and Figley C.R. (2004) 'Development and validation of the Secondary Traumatic Stress Scale', *Research on Social Work Practice*, 14: 27–35.

Brown, J., Fielding J., and Grover J. (1999) 'Distinguishing traumatic, vicarious and routine operational stressor exposure and attendant adverse consequences in a sample of police officers', *Work & Stress*, 13(4): 312–25.

Bryant, R. (2018) 'Innate reasoning and critical incident decision-making', in M. Roycroft and J. Roach (eds) *Decision-making in Police Enquiries and Critical Incidents: What Really Works?* London: Palgrave Macmillan, pp 47–67.

Burns, C.M., Morley, J., Bradshaw, R. et al (2008) 'The emotional impact on and coping strategies employed by police teams investigating internet child exploitation', *Traumatology*, 14(2): 20–31.

Byford, L. (1981) *The Yorkshire Ripper Case: Review of the police investigation of the case.* Available at https://www.gov.uk/government/publications/sir-lawrence-byford-report-into-the-police handling-of-the-yorkshire-ripper-case (accessed 20 October 2022).

Canter, D. (1994) *Criminal Shadows: In the Mind of the Serial Killer*, London: HarperCollins.

Cartwright, A. and Roach, J. (2021a) 'A price paid? A review of the research on the impact of investigating serious crime on the wellbeing of police staff', *The Police Journal: Theory, Practice and Principles*, 95(1): 109–26.

Cartwright, A. and Roach, J. (2021b) 'The wellbeing of UK police: a study of recorded absences from work of UK police employees due to psychological illness and stress using Freedom of Information Act data', *Policing: A Journal of Policy and Practice*, 15(2): 1326–38.

Chenery, S., Henshaw, C., and Pease, K. (1999) *Illegal Parking in Disabled Bays: A Means of Offender Targeting, Policing and Reducing Crime Briefing Note 1/99*, London: Home Office.

Clarke, R.V.G. (1980) 'Situational Crime Prevention: theory and practice', *British Journal of Criminology*, 20(2): 136–47.

Clarke, R.V.G. (ed) (1997) *Situational Crime Prevention: Successful Studies* (2nd edn), Albany, NY: Harrow and Heston.

Cohen, L. and Felson, M. (1979) 'Social change and crime rate trends: a routine activity approach', *American Sociological Review*, 44: 588–608.

Cohen, L. and Felson, M. (2008) 'The routine activity approach', in R. Wortley and L. Mazerolle (eds) *Environmental Criminology and Crime Analysis*, Cullompton: Willan.

Colls, J., Hall, H.V., and Poirier, J. (2001) *Deception and Nonverbal Behavior*, New York: CRC Press.

Cornish, D.B. and Clarke, R.V. (1986) (eds) *The Reasoning Criminal*, New York: Springer-Verlag.

Cornish, D.B. and Clarke, R.V. (2003) 'Opportunities, precipitators and criminal decisions: a reply to Wortley's critique of Situational Crime Prevention', in M.J. Smith and D.B. Cornish (eds) *Theory and Practice in Situational Crime Prevention*, Vol 16, Monsey, NY: Criminal Justice Press, pp 111–24.

Cornish, D.B. and Clarke, R.V. (2006) 'The rational choice perspective', in S. Henry and M.M. Lanier (eds) *The Essential Criminology Reader*, Boulder, CO: Westview Press, pp 38–51.

Cornish, D.B. and Clarke, R.V. (2008) 'The rational choice perspective', in R. Wortley and L. Mazerolle (eds) *Environmental Criminology and Crime Analysis*, Uffculme: Willan, pp 21–47.

Crandall, B.W., Kyne, M., Miltello, L., and Klein, G. (1992) 'Describing expertise in one-on-one instruction (Contract MDA903-91-C-0058)', for the US Army Research Institute, Alexandria, VA and Fairborn, OH: Klein Associates.

Craun, S.W, Bourke, M.L., and Coulson, F.N. (2015) 'The impact of internet crimes against children work on relationships with families and friends: an exploratory study', *Journal of Family Violence*, 30: 393–402.

Cunliffe, J. and Shepherd, A. (2007) 'Re-offending of adults: results from the 2004 cohort', Home Office Statistical Bulletin 06/04, London: Home office.

Davies, M., Smith, R., and Rogers, P. (2009) 'Police perceptions of rape as a function of victim gender and sexuality', *The Police Journal: Theory, Practice and Principles*, 82(1): 4–12.

Delmas, H., Elissalde, B., Rochat, N., Demarchi, S., Tijus, C., and Urdapilleta, I. (2019) 'Policemen's and civilians' beliefs about facial cues of deception', *Journal of Nonverbal Behavior*, 43(1): 59–90.

DePaulo, B.M., Lindsay, J.J., Malone, B.E., Muhlenbruck, L., Charlton, K., and Cooper, H. (2003) 'Cues to deception', *Psychological Bulletin*, 129(1): 74–112.

Donnelly, D. and West, A. (2018) 'The task is greater than the title: professionalising the role of the Senior Investigating Officer in Homicide investigations', in M. Roycroft, and J. Roach (eds) *Decision-making in Police Enquiries and Critical Incidents: What Really Works?* London: Palgrave Macmillan, pp 107–28.

Duckworth, D.H. (1991) 'Facilitating recovery from disaster-work experiences', *British Journal of Guidance & Counselling*, 19(1): 13–22.

Ekblom, P. (2000) 'Going equipped', *British Journal of Criminology*, 40(3): 376–98.

Ekman, P. (1988) 'Lying and nonverbal behavior: theoretical issues and new findings', *Journal of Nonverbal Behavior*, 12(3): 163–75.

Ericsson, K.A. (2006a) 'An introduction to *The Cambridge Handbook of Expertise and Expert Performance*: its development, organization and content', in K.A. Ericsson, N. Charness, P. Feltovich, and R. Hoffman (eds) *The Cambridge Handbook of Expertise and Expert Performance*, New York: Cambridge University Press, pp 3–21.

Ericsson, K.A. (2006b) 'Expertise', *Current Biology*, 24(11).

Everson, S. and Pease, K. (2001) 'Crime against the same person and place: detection opportunity and offender targeting', in G. Farrell and K. Pease (eds) *Repeat Victimization*, Monsey, NY: Criminal Justice Press, pp 199–220.

Fahsing, I. (2018) 'The making of an expert detective: a European perspective – comparing decision-making in Norway and UK', in M. Roycroft and J. Roach (eds) *Decision-making in Police Enquiries and Critical Incidents: What Really Works?* London: Palgrave Macmillan, pp 83–105.

Fahsing, I. and Ask, K. (2013) 'Decision-making and decisional tipping points in homicide investigations: an interview study of British and Norwegian detectives', *Journal of Investigative Psychology and Offender Profiling*, 10(2): 155–65.

Fahsing, I. and Ask, K. (2016) 'The making of an expert detective: the role of experience in English and Norwegian police officers' investigative decision-making', *Psychology, Crime & Law*, 22(3): 203–23.

Farrell, G. and Brown, R. (2016) 'On the origins of the crime drop: vehicle crime and security in the 1980s', *The Howard Journal*, 55(1–2): 1–12.

Farrell, G. and Pease, K. (1993) 'Once bitten, twice bitten: repeat victimisation and its implications for crime prevention', *Police Research Group Crime Prevention Unit Series Paper no. 46*, London: Home Office Police Department.

Farrell, G. and Pease, K. (2017) 'Preventing repeat and near repeat crime concentrations', in N. Tilley and A. Sidebottom (eds) *Handbook of Crime Prevention and Community Safety* (2nd edn), London: Routledge, pp 143–56.

Farrington, D.P. (1986) 'Age and crime', *Crime and Justice*, 7: 189–250.

Farrington, D.P. and Hawkins, J.D. (1991) 'Predicting participation, early onset, and later persistence in officially recorded offending', *Criminal Behaviour and Mental Health*, 1(1): 1–33.

Farrington, D.P., Snyder, H.N., and Finnegan, T.A. (1988) 'Specialisation in juvenile court careers', *Criminology*, 26(3): 461–87.

Farrington, D.P., Coid, J.W., Harnett, L. et al (2006) 'Criminal careers and life success: new findings from the Cambridge Study in Delinquent Development', *Home Office Findings Paper 281*, London: Home Office. Available at http://www.crim.cam.ac.uk/people/academic_research/david_farrington/hofind281.pdf (accessed 8 October 2015).

Felson, M. (1994) *Crime and Everyday Life*, Thousand Oaks, CA: Pine Forge Press.

Felson, M. (1998) *Crime and Everyday Life* (2nd edn), Thousand Oaks, CA: Pine Forge Press.

Felson, M. and Clarke, R.V. (1998) 'Opportunity makes the thief: practical theory for crime prevention', *Police Research paper 98*, Policing and Reducing Crime Unit, Research, Development and Statistics Directorate, UK Home Office.

Figley, C.R. (1995) 'Compassion fatigue: toward a new understanding of the costs of caring', in B.H. Stamm (ed) *Secondary Traumatic Stress: Self-Care Issues for Clinicians, Researchers, and Educators*, Derwood, MD: The Sidran Press, pp 3–28.

Figley, C.R. (2002) 'Compassion fatigue: psychotherapists' chronic lack of self care', *Journal of Clinical Psychology*, 58(11): 1433–41.

Finn, P. and Tomz, J.E. (1996) *Developing a Law Enforcement Stress Program for Officers and Their Spouses*, Washington, DC: National Institute of Justice.

Flanagan, R. (2008) *A Review of Policing: Final Report. Independent Review of Policing*. Available at: http://webarchive.nationalarchives.gov.uk/20080910134927/police.homeoffice.gov.uk/publications/police-reform/review_of_policing_final_report/ (accessed 8 October 2021).

Foley, J. and Massey, K. (2019) 'Police officers and post-traumatic stress disorder: discussing the deficit in research, identification and prevention in England and Wales', *The Police Journal: Theory, Practice and Principles*, 92(1): 23–34.

Foley, J., Hassett, A., and Williams, E. (2021) 'Getting on with the job: a systemised literature review of secondary trauma and post-traumatic stress disorder (PTSD) in policing within the United Kingdom (UK)', *The Police Journal: Theory, Practice and Principles*. Advanced access available at https://journals-sagepub-com.libaccess.hud.ac.uk/doi/pdf/10.1177/0032258X21990412 (accessed 21 January 2022).

Fyhn, T., Fjell, K., and Johnsen, B. (2016) 'Resilience factors among police investigators: hardiness-commitment a unique contributor', *Journal of Police and Criminal Psychology*, 31: 261–9.

Geiselman, R.E., Fisher, R.P., MacKinnon, D.P., and Holland, H.L. (1985) 'Eyewitness memory enhancement in the police interview: cognitive retrieval mnemonics versus hypnosis', *Journal of Applied Psychology*, 70(2): 401–12.

Gibson, J.J. (1966) *The Senses Considered as Perceptual Systems*, London: Allen and Unwin.

Gibson, J.J. (1975) 'Affordances and behavior', in E.S. Reed and R. Jones (eds) *Reasons for Realism: Selected Essays of James J. Gibson* (1st edn), Hillsdale, NJ: Lawrence Erlbaum, pp 410–11.

Goldstein, H. (1977) 'Policing a free society', *Legal Studies Research Paper No. 1349*, Wisconsin, WI: Ballinger, University of Wisconsin. Available at: http://ssrn.com/abstract=2596883 (accessed 6 July 2018).

Goldstein, H. (2018) 'On problem-oriented policing: the Stockholm Lecture', *Journal of Crime Science*, 7 (13): 1–10.

Goldstein, H. and Susmilch, C. (1982) 'Experimenting with the problem-oriented approach to improving police service: a report and some reflections on two case studies', Photocopy of vol 4 of the project on development of a problem-oriented approach to improving police service, Madison, WI: University of Wisconsin Law School. Available at: http://www.popcenter.org/library/researcherprojects/DevelopmentofPOPVolIV.pdf (accessed 6 July 2018).

Gollwitzer, P.M. (1990) 'Action phases and mindsets', in E.T. Higgins (ed) *Handbook of Motivation and Cognition: Foundations of Social Behaviour*, Vol 2, New York: Guilford Press, pp 53–92.

Gollwitzer, P.M., Heckhausen, H., and Steller, B. (1990) 'Deliberative and implemental mindsets: cognitive tuning towards congruous thoughts and information', *Journal of Personality and Social Psychology*, 59(6): 1119–27.

Goodman-Delahunty, J. and Graham, K. (2011) 'The influence of victim intoxication and victim attire on police response to sexual assault', *Journal of Investigative Psychology and Offender Profiling*, 8(1): 22–40.

Gottfredson, M. and Hirshi, T. (1990) *A General Theory of Crime*, Stanford, CA: Stanford University Press.

Granhag, P.A., Vrij, A., and Verschuere, B. (2014) *Detecting Deception: Current Challenges and Cognitive Approaches*, Chichester: Wiley.

Gray, C. and Rydon-Grange, M. (2019) 'Individual characteristics, secondary trauma and burnout in police sexual and violent offending teams', *The Police Journal: Theory, Practice and Principles*, 93(2): 146–61.

Greenall, P.V. and Wright, M. (2015) 'Exploring the criminal histories of stranger sexual killers', *The Journal of Forensic Psychiatry and Psychology*, 26(2): 249–59.

Greenberg, N., Brooks, S., and Dunn, R. (2015) 'Latest developments in posttraumatic stress disorder: diagnosis and treatment', *British Medical Bulletin*, 114(1): 1–9.

Gross, R. (1996) *Psychology: The Science of Mind and Behaviour* (3rd edn), Abingdon: Hodder and Stoughton.

Hamilton-Smith, N. and Kent, A. (2005) 'Preventing domestic burglary', in N. Tilley (ed) *Handbook of Crime Prevention and Community Safety*, Collumpton: Willan, pp 143–70.

Harris, D.A., Smallbone, S., Dennison, S., and Knight, R.A. (2009) 'Specialisation and versatility in sexual offenders referred for civil commitment', *Journal of Criminal Justice*, 37: 37–44.

Hart, P.M., Wearing, A.J., and Headey, B. (1993) 'Police stress and well-being: integrating personality, coping and daily work experiences', *Journal of Occupational Psychology*, 68: 133–57.

Hawkins, H.C. (2001) 'Police officer burnout: a partial replication of Maslach's Burnout Inventory', *Police Quarterly*, 4: 343–60.

He, N., Zhao, J., and Archbold, C. (2002) 'Gender and police stress', *Policing: An International Journal of Police Strategies & Management*, 25(4): 687–708.

Hirschfeld, A. (2004) 'The impact of the reducing burglary initiative in the north of England', *Home Office Online Report 40/04*, London: Home Office.

Hirschfeld, A., Newton, A., and Rogerson, M. (2010) 'Linking burglary and target hardening at the property level: new insights into victimization and burglary protection', *Criminal Justice Policy Review*, 21(3): 319–37.

Hobbs, D. (1998) *Doing the Business: Entrepreneurship, Detectives and the Working Class in the East End of London*, Oxford: Oxford University Press.

Horswell, J. and Fowler, C. (2004) 'Associative evidence: the Locard exchange principle', in J. Horswell (ed) *The Practice of Crime Scene Investigation*, Boca Raton: CRC Press, pp 77–8.

Huey, L. and Broll, R. (2015) '"I don't find it sexy at all": criminal investigators' views of media glamorization of police "dirty work"', *Policing and Society: An International Journal of Research and Policy*, 25(2): 236–47.

James, A. and Mills, M. (2012) 'Does ACPO know best: to what extent may the PIP programme provide a template for the professionalising of policing?', *The Police Journal: Theory, Practice and Principles*, 85(2): 133–49.

Kahneman, D. (1973) *Attention and Effort*, New Jersey: Citeseer.

Kahneman, D. (2011) *Thinking Fast and Slow*, London: Allen Lane.

Kahneman, D., Slovic, P., and Tversky, A. (eds) (1982) *Judgement Under Uncertainty: Heuristics and Biases*, Cambridge: Cambridge University Press.

Kelling, G. and Coles, C. (1995) *Fixing Broken Windows*, New York: Free Press.

Kelty, S.F. and Gordon, H. (2015) 'No burnout at this coal-face: managing occupational stress in forensic personnel and the implications for forensic and criminal justice agencies', *Psychiatry, Psychology and Law*, 22(2): 273–90.

Kempf, K. (1987) 'Specialisation and the criminal career', *Criminology*, 25(2): 399–420.

Klein, G.A. and Hoffmann, R. (1993) 'Seeing the invisible: perceptual/cognitive aspects of expertise', in M. Rabinowitz (ed) *Cognitive Science Foundations of Instruction*, Mahwah, NJ: Lawrence Erlbaum Associates, pp 203–26.

Kobasa, C., Maddi, R., and Kahn, S. (1982) 'Hardiness and health: a prospective study', *Journal of Personality and Social Psychology*, 42(1): 168–77.

Kohan, A. and O'Connor, B.P. (2002) 'Police officer job satisfaction in relation to mood, well-being, and alcohol consumption', *Journal of Psychology*, 136(3): 307–19.

Kurtz, D.L. (2008) 'Controlled burn: the gendering of stress and burnout in modern policing', *Feminist Criminology*, 3(3): 216–38.

Lazarus, R.S. and Folkman, S. (1984) *Stress, Appraisal, and Coping*, New York: Springer.

LeBlanc, M. and Frechette, M. (1989) *Male Criminal Activity from Childhood Through Youth: Multilevel and Developmental Perspectives*, New York: Springer-Verlag.

Leins, D.A., Fisher, R.P., and Ross, S.J. (2013) 'Exploring liars' strategies for creating deceptive reports', *Legal and Criminological Psychology*, 18(1): 141–51.

Liberman, A.M., Best, S.R., Metzler, T.J., Fagan, J.A., Weiss, D.S., and Marmar, C.R. (2002) 'Routine occupational stress and psychological distress in police', *Policing: An International Journal of Police Strategic & Management*, 25: 421–41.

MacEachern, A.D., Jindal-Snape, D., and Jackson, S. (2011) 'Child abuse investigation: police officers and secondary traumatic stress', *International Journal of Occupational Safety and Ergonomics*, 17(4): 329–39.

MacEachern, A.D., Dennis, A.A., and Jackson, S. (2018) 'Secondary traumatic stress: prevalence and symptomology among detective officers investigating child protection cases', *Journal of Police and Criminal Psychology*, 34(2): 165–74.

Macquet, A.C. (2009) 'Recognition within the decision-making process: a case study of expert volleyball players', *Journal of Applied Sport Psychology*, 21(1): 64–79.

Maguire, M. (2008) 'Criminal investigation and crime control', in T. Newburn (ed) *Handbook of Policing* (2nd edn), Cullompton: Willan, pp 430–65.

Maple, J. (1999) *Crime Fighter*, New York: Broadway Books.

Masip, J., Blandón-Gitlin, I., Martínez, C., Herrero, C., and Ibabe, I. (2016) 'Strategic interviewing to detect deception: cues to deception across repeated interviews', *Frontiers in Psychology*, 7(1): 1701–2.

Matthews, R., Pease, C., and Pease, K. (2001) *Repeated Bank Robbery: Themes and Variations*, New Jersey: Criminal Justice Press.

Mazerolle, P., Brame, R., Paternoster, R., Piquero, A., and Dean, C. (2000) 'Onset age, persistence, and offending versatility: comparisons across gender', *Criminology*, 38(4): 1143–72.

McCann, I.L. and Pearlman, L.A. (1990) 'Vicarious traumatization: a framework for understanding the psychological effects of working with victims', *Journal of Traumatic Stress*, 3(1): 131–49.

McCartney, C. (2006) *Forensic Identification and Criminal Justice: Forensic Science, Justice and Risk*, Cullompton: Willan.

Memon, A., Meissner, C.A., and Fraser, J. (2010) 'The cognitive interview: a meta-analytic review and study space analysis of the past 25 years', *Psychology, Public Policy, and Law*, 16(4): 340–72.

MINDSPACE (2010) Influencing behaviour through public policy. UK Cabinet Office and Institute for Government. Available at: https://www.bi.team/publications/mindspace/ (accessed 21 February 2021).

Mokros, A. and Alison, L.J. (2002) 'Is offender profiling possible? Testing the predicted homology of crime scene actions and background characteristics in a sample of rapists', *Legal and Criminological Psychology*, 7(1): 25–43.

Nee, C. and Meenaghan, A. (2006) 'Expert decision-making in burglars', *British Journal of Criminology*, 46(5): 935–49.

Nettle, D., Nott, K., and Bateson, M. (2012) '"Cycle thieves, we are watching you": impact of a simple signage intervention against bicycle theft', *PLoS ONE*, 7(12). https://doi.org/10.1371/journal.pone.00517 38

Newell, J.M. and MacNeil, G.A. (2010) 'Professional burnout, vicarious trauma, secondary traumatic stress, and compassion fatigue: a review of theoretical terms, risk factors, and preventive methods for clinicians and researchers', *Best Practices in Mental Health*, 6(2): 57–68.

Nho, S.M. and Kim, E.A. (2017) 'Factors influencing post traumatic stress disorder in crime scene investigators', *Journal of Korean Academy of Nursing*, 47(1): 39.

Norman, D. (1998) *The Design of Everyday Things*, London: MIT Press.

Nortje, A. and Tredoux, C. (2019) 'How good are we at detecting deception? A review of current techniques and theories', *South African Journal of Psychology*, 49(4): 491–504.

Padyab, M., Backteman-Erlanson, S., and Brulin, C. (2016) 'Burnout, coping, stress of conscience and psychosocial work environment among patrolling police officers', *Journal of Police and Criminal Psychology*, 31: 229–37.

Page, A.D. (2008a) 'Gateway to reform: policy implications of police officers' attitudes towards rape', *American Journal of Criminal Justice*, 33(1): 44–58.

Page, A.D. (2008b) 'Judging women and defining crime: police officers' attitudes towards women and rape', *Sociological Spectrum*, 28(4): 389–411.

Page, A.D. (2010) 'True colours: police officers and rape myth acceptance', *Feminist Criminology*, 5(4): 315–34.

Parkes, R., Graham-Kevan, N., and Bryce, J. (2019) 'You don't see the world through the same eyes anymore: the impact of sexual offending work on police staff', *The Police Journal: Theory, Practice and Principles*, 92(4): 316–38.

Pavšič Mrevlje, T. (2016) 'Coping with work-related traumatic situations among crime scene technicians', *Stress and Health*, 32(4): 374–82.

Pease, K. (1998) 'Repeat victimization: taking stock', *Crime Prevention & Detection Paper 90*, London: Home Office.

Pease K. (2006) 'No through road: closing pathways to crime', in K. Moss and M. Stephens (eds) *Crime Reduction and the Law*, Abingdon: Routledge, pp 50–67.

Pease, K., Ignatans, D., and Batty, L. (2018) 'Whatever happened to repeat victimisation?', *Crime Prevention and Community Safety*, 20: 256–67.

Perez, L.M., Jones, J., Englert, D.R. et al (2010) 'Secondary traumatic stress and burnout among law enforcement investigators exposed to disturbing media images', *Journal of Police and Criminal Psychology*, 25(2): 113–24.

Pinker, S. (2011) *The Better Angels of Our Nature: Why Violence Has Declined*, New York: Viking.

Piquero, A. (2000) 'Frequency, specialisation, and violence in offending careers', *Journal of Research in Crime and Delinquency*, 37(4): 392–418.

Polanyi, M. (1966) *The Tacit Dimension*, Chicago, IL: University of Chicago Press.

Ratcliffe, J. (2009) *Intelligence-Led Policing*, Cullompton: Willan.

Ratcliffe, J. (2016) *Intelligence-Led Policing* (2nd edn), London: Routledge.

Ressler, R., Burgess, A., Douglas, J., Hartman, C., and D'Agostino, R. (1986) 'Murderers who rape and mutiliate', *Journal of Interpersonal Violence*, 1(3): 273–87.

Roach, J. (2007a) 'Those who do big bad things also usually do little bad things: identifying active serious offenders using offender self-selection', *International Journal of Police Science and Management*, 9(1): 66–79.

Roach, J. (2007b) 'HO/RT1culture: cultivating police use of Home Office Road Traffic 1 form to identify active serious offenders', *International Journal of Police Science and Management*, 9(4): 357–70.

Roach, J. (2010) 'Home is where the heart lies? A study of false address giving to police', *Legal and Criminological Psychology*, 15(2): 209–20.

Roach, J. (2012) 'Terrorists, affordance and the over-estimation of offence homogeneity', in M. Taylor and P.M. Currie (eds) *Terrorism and Affordance*, London: Continuum, pp 141–56.

Roach, J. (2017) 'Self-Selection Policing and the disqualified driver', *Policing: A Journal of Policy and Practice*, 13(3): 300–11.

Roach, J. (2018) 'Those who do big bad things still do little bad things: re-stating the case for self-selection policing', in R. Wortley, A. Sidebottom, N. Tilley, and G. Laycock (eds) *Routledge Handbook of Crime Science*, Abingdon: Routledge, pp 320–33.

Roach, J. and Bryant, R. (2015) 'Child homicide: generating victim and suspect risk profiles', *Journal of Criminal Psychology*, 5(3): 201–15.

Roach, J. and Pease, K. (2006) 'DNA evidence and police investigations: a health warning', *Police Professional*, 52.

Roach, J. and Pease, K. (2009) 'Necropsies and the cold case', in D.K. Rossmo (ed) *Criminal Investigative Failures*, Boca Raton: CRC Press, pp 327–48.

Roach, J. and Pease, K. (2013) 'Police overestimation of criminal career homogeneity', *Journal of Investigative Psychology and Offender Profiling*, 11(2): 164–78.

Roach, J. and Pease, K. (2016) *Self-Selection Policing: Theory, Research and Practice*, Basingstoke, Hampshire: Palgrave Macmillan.

Roach, J. and Selby-Fell, H. (forthcoming) 'Psychology and policing', in K. Corteen, R. Steele, N. Cross, and M. McManus (eds) *Forensic Psychology, Crime and Policing: Key Issues and Practical Debates*, Bristol: Policy Press.

Roach, J., Alexander, R., and Pease, K. (2012) 'Signal crimes and signal policing', *The Police Journal*, 85(2): 161–8.

Roach, J., Pease, K., and Clegg, K. (2011) 'Stars in their lies: how better to identify people who give false dates of birth to police', *Policing: A Journal of Policy and Practice*, 5(1): 56–64.

Roach, J., Weir, K., Phillips, P., Gaskell, K., and Walton, M. (2016) 'Nudging down theft from insecure vehicles: a pilot study', *International Journal of Police Science and Management*, 19(1): 31–8.

Roach, J., Sharratt, K., Cartwright, A. et al (2018) 'Cognitive and emotional stressors of child homicide investigations on UK and Danish police investigators', *Homicide Studies*, 22(3): 296–320.

Rose, G. (2000) 'The criminal histories of serious traffic offenders', *Home Office Research Study number 206*, London: Home Office.

Ross, L. (1977) 'The intuitive psychologist and his shortcomings: distortions in the attribution process', in L. Berkowitz (ed) *Advances in Experimental Social Psychology*, Vol 10, New York: Academic Press, pp 173–220.

Ross, K.G., Shafer, J.L., and Klein, G. (2006) 'Professional judgments and "naturalistic decision-making"', in K.A. Ericsson, N. Charness, P. Feltovich, and R. Hoffman (eds) *The Cambridge Handbook of Expertise and Expert Performance*, New York: Cambridge University Press, pp 402–19.

Rossmo, D.K. (ed) (2009) *Criminal Investigative Failures*, Boca Raton: CRC Press.

Rotter, J.B. (1966) 'Generalized expectancies for internal versus external control of reinforcement', *Psychological Monographs: General and Applied*, 80(1): 1–28.

Rouse, W.B. and Morris, N.M. (1986) 'On looking into the black box: prospects and limits on the search for mental models', *Psychological Bulletin*, 100(3): 349–63.

Roycroft, M. and Roach, J. (eds) (2019) *Decision-making in Police Enquiries and Critical Incidents: What Really Works?* London: Palgrave Macmillan.

Salfati, C.G. and Bateman, A.L. (2005) 'Serial homicide: an investigation of behavioural consistency', *Journal of Investigative Psychology and Offender Profiling*, 2(2): 121–44.

Salo, I. and Allwood, C.M. (2011) 'Decision-making styles, stress and gender among investigators', *Policing: An International Journal of Police Strategies & Management*, 34(1): 97–119.

Sherman, L.W. (1998) *Evidence-Based Policing*, Washington, DC: Police Foundation.

Sherman, L.W. (2013) 'The rise of evidence-based policing: targeting, testing and tracking', *Crime and Justice*, 42: 377–451.

Schneider, J.L. (2005) 'The link between shoplifting and burglary: the booster burglar', *British Journal of Criminology*, 45(3): 395–401.

Schuller, R.A. and Stewart, A. (2000) 'Police responses to sexual assault complaints: the role of perpetrator/complainant intoxication', *Law and Human Behavior*, 24(5): 535–51.

Sharma, D. and Kilgallon-Scott, M. (2015) 'Shopping mall design could nudge shoplifters into doing the right thing – here's how', *The Conversation*, 4 June. Available at: https://theconversation.com/shoppingmall-design-could-nudge-shoplifters-intodoing-the-right-thing-heres-how-42292 (accessed 1 September 2016).

Sidebottom, A., Tompson, L., Thornton, A. et al (2017) 'Gating alleys to reduce crime: a meta-analysis and realist synthesis', *Justice Quarterly* 35(1): 55–86.

Simon, D. (2012) *In Doubt: The Psychology of the Criminal Justice Process*, Cambridge, MA: Harvard University Press.

Sleath, E. and Bull, R. (2012) 'Comparing rape victim and perpetrator blaming in a police officer sample: differences between police officers with and without special training', *Criminal Justice and Behavior*, 39(5): 646–65.

Sleath, E. and Bull, R. (2017) 'Police perceptions of rape victims and the impact on case decision-making: a systematic review', *Aggression and Violent Behavior*, 34: 102–12.

Smerdon, J. and South, N. (1997) 'Deviant drivers and moral hazards: risk, no insurance, offending and some suggestions for policy and practice', *International Journal of Risk, Security and Crime Prevention*, 2(4): 27–90.

Smith, N. and Flanagan, C. (2000) 'The effective detective: identifying the skills of an effective SIO', *Police Research Series Paper 122*, London: Policing and Reducing Crime Unit.

Sollie, H., Kop, N., and Euwema, M.C. (2017) 'Mental resilience of crime scene investigators: how police officers perceive and cope with the impact of demanding work situations', *Criminal Justice and Behavior*, 44(12): 1580–603.

Soothill, K., Francis, B., Sanderson, B., and Ackerley, E. (2000) 'Sex offenders: specialists, generalists or both?', *British Journal of Criminology*, 40(1): 56–67.

Soothill, K., Fitzpatrick, C., and Francis, B. (2009) *Understanding Criminal Careers*, Cullompton: Willan.

Steer, D.J. and Car-Hill, R.A. (1967) 'The motoring offender: who is he?', *Criminal Law Review*, 214–24.

Stelfox, P. (2008) *Criminal Investigation*, Cullompton: Willan.

Stevenson, J. (2007) 'Welfare considerations for supervisors managing child sexual abuse on-line units', MSc Thesis. Available at: https://www.shiftwellness.net/wp-content/uploads/2016/05/ Bound-Bramshill-Study-2007.pdf (accessed January 2020).

Suggs, D. (1998) 'Motor projects in England and Wales: an evaluation', *Home Office Research, Development and Statistics Directorate, Research Findings No. 81*, London: Home Office.

Taris, W., Kompier, J., Geurts, E., Houtman, D., and van den Heuvel, M. (2010) 'Professional efficacy, exhaustion, and work characteristics among police officers: a longitudinal test of the learning-related predictions of the demand-control model', *Journal of Occupational and Organizational Psychology*, 83(2): 455–74.

Tarling, R. (1993) *Analysing Offending: Data, Models and Interpretations*, London: HMSO.

Tehrani, N. (2016) 'Extraversion, neuroticism and secondary trauma in internet child abuse investigators', *Occupational Medicine*, 66(5): 403–7.

Thaler, R. and Sunstein, C.R. (2008) *Nudge: Improving Decisions about Health, Wealth, and Happiness*, London: Penguin.

Townsley, M. and Pease, K. (2003) 'Two go wild in Knowsley: analysis for evidence-led crime reduction', in K. Bullock and N. Tilley (eds) *Problem-Orientated Policing*, Cullompton: Willan, pp 22–34.

Tseloni, A. and Pease, K. (2003) 'Repeat personal victimization: "boosts" or "flags"?', *British Journal of Criminology*, 43(1): 196–212.

Tversky, A. and Kahneman, D. (1992) 'Advances in prospect theory: cumulative representation of uncertainty', *Journal of Risk and Uncertainty*, 5(4): 297–323.

Van Patten, I.T. and Burke, T.W. (2001) 'Critical incident stress and the child homicide investigator', *Homicide Studies*, 5(2): 131–52.

Venema, R.M. (2014) 'Police officer schema of sexual assault reports: real rape, ambiguous cases, and false reports', *Journal of Interpersonal Violence*, 31(5): 872–99.

Violanti, J. (2005) 'Dying for the job: psychological stress, disease and mortality in police work', in K. Copes (ed) *Policing and Stress*, Upper Saddle River, NJ: Prentice Hall, pp 78–95.

Violanti, J., Charles, L., McCanlies, E. et al (2017) 'Police stressors and health: a state-of-the-art review', *Policing: An International Journal of Police Strategies & Management*, 40: 642–56.

Vogl, S. and Vogl, S. (2015) 'Children's verbal, interactive and cognitive skills and implications for interviews', *Quality & Quantity*, 49(1): 319–38.

Vrij, A. (2008) *Detecting Lies and Deceit: Pitfalls and Opportunities* (2nd edn), New York: John Wiley & Sons.

Vrij, A. (2014) 'Interviewing to detect deception', *European Psychologist*, 19(3): 184–94.

Vrij, A. and Semin, G.R. (1996) 'Lie experts' beliefs about nonverbal indicators of deception', *Journal of Nonverbal Behavior*, 20(1): 65–80.

Vrij, A., Leal, S., Granhag, P.A. et al (2009) 'Outsmarting the liars: the benefit of asking unanticipated questions', *Law and Human Behavior*, 33(2): 159–66.

Walsh, A. and Ellis, L. (2007) *Criminology: An Interdisciplinary Approach*, Thousand Oaks, CA: Sage.

Weisburd, D., Farrington, D., and Gill, C. (2017) 'What works in crime prevention and rehabilitation', *Criminology & Public Policy*, 16(2): 415–49.

Wellsmith, M. and Guille, H. (2005) 'Fixed penalty notices as a means of offender selection', *International Journal of Police Science and Management*, 7(1): 36–44.

Willett, T.C. (1964) *Criminal on the Road: A Study of Serious Motoring Offences and Those Who Commit Them*, London: Tavistock Publications.

Wilson, J.Q. and Kelling, G.L. (1982) 'Broken windows: the police and neighbourhood safety', *Atlantic Monthly*, March: 29–38.

Woodhams, J., Grant, T.D., and Price, A.R.G. (2007) 'From marine ecology to crime analysis: improving the detection of serial sexual offences using a taxonomic similarity measure', *Journal of Investigative Psychology and Offender Profiling*, 4(3): 17–27.

Wortley, R., Sidebottom, A., Tilley, N., and Laycock, G. (eds) (2019) *Routledge Handbook of Crime Science*, Abingdon: Routledge.

Wright, M. (2013) 'Homicide detectives' intuition', *Journal of Investigative Psychology and Offender Profiling*, 10(2): 182–99.

Yarbrough, J.R. (2020) 'The science of deception detection: a literature and policy review on police ability to detect lies', *Journal of Criminal Justice and Law*, 3(2): 40–58.

Yoo, Y.-S., Cho, O.-H., Cha, K.-S. et al (2013) 'Factors influencing post-traumatic stress in Korean forensic science investigators', *Asian Nursing Research*, 7(3): 136–41.

Zimbardo, P.G. (1973) 'A field experiment in auto-shaping', in C. Ward (ed) *Vandalism*, London: Architectural Press.

Zimbardo, P.G. (2007) *The Lucifer Effect: Understanding How Good People Turn Evil*, New York: Random House.

Zuckerman, M. and Driver, R.E. (1985) 'Telling lies: verbal and nonverbal correlates of deception', in A.W. Siegman and S. Feldstein (eds) *Multi-Channel Integrations of Non-Verbal Behavior*, Hillsdale, NJ: Erlbaum, pp 129–47.

Zuckerman, M., DePaulo, B.M., and Rosenthal, R. (1981) 'Verbal and non-verbal communication of deception', in L. Berkowitz (ed) *Advances in Experimental and Social Psychology*, Vol 14, New York: Academic Press, pp 1–59.

Index

References to figures appear in *italic* type; those in **bold** type refer to tables. References to endnotes show both the page number and the note number (115n1).

R

S

T

U

V

W

Y

Z